HOWUL
A LIFE'S JOURNEY

HOWUL

A LIFE'S JOURNEY

DAVID SHANNON

Elsewhen Press

HOWUL

First published in Great Britain by Elsewhen Press, 2021
An imprint of Alnpete Limited

Elsewhen Press, PO Box 757, Dartford, Kent DA2 7TQ
www.elsewhen.press
British Library Cataloguing in Publication Data.
A catalogue record for this book is available from the British Library.
ISBN 978-1-911409-80-9 Print edition
ISBN 978-1-911409-90-8 eBook edition

Printed and bound by CPI Group (UK) Ltd, Croydon, CR0 4YY

For the many free-flowing, majestic Shannons there have been in my life and also, of course, for the mighty, magnificent B.

CONTENTS

BEGIN

Simple time keep people simple. This, that, be happy, be sad. Take books away, heads have less clutter. Take food away, everyone do as they is ask.

Well, not everyone. Not alway.

All of next is only what Howul have tell me or write.

What is true? What is billy bully? I still have not the foggyrest.

#

BLANOW

Since he is knee high to a grasshop, everyone tell him books is dangerous. If you read them, they fill your head with dribble. You cannot eat them and when you throw them in the fire, they give bad heat.

The book he hold now smell like old mushrooms. On its bright pink front is two snotnoses of People Before. The pages is stick together with black glop and dead insects. As he peel them back, he see words write down on them. He close the book and look at it like it give him disease.

He hear a hiss and cough. This is how Gommel laugh.

'Today I start to learn you how to read and write,' he say.

Gommel is the most old man in Blanow. Hims legs is twigs of rosemary, hims face is bark of olive tree, hims hair is wood smoke. Hims house is so near the back cliffs that slates oft time crash onto its roof. Hims deaf ears never hear them.

Gommel sit now in a big People Before leather chair in the room he hardly ever leave. All hims furniture is People Before. Big wood table. Three hard wood chairs for those who sit with him, make him dandelion tea, bring him tinfoods. A bed with thick blankets and a cushion for hims head. Candles and lamps on wood stands. Wood plates, dishes, spoons. Nothing brack nor botch. All good.

The heavy wood stick he walk with rest against hims legs. He use both hands to hold it there because hims stiff fingers do not full close. Hims green shirt is People Before and press tight against hims fine plumpy stomach. Hims grey britches is also People Before and soft grip hims thin legs like skin of catterpilly.

Most of what Howul have is brack and botch. Hims shirt is make from leafs, hims britches from beech bark, hims shoes from pine bark. All is itch and scratch and chafe. At thirty five year, he still run most fast and see most sharp of all in Blanow. Hims face is also most grumpscrut. Since he is snotnose, even when hims thinkings is sweet and kind, everyone still think he wish them pain.

Since Jen die, he now leave sweet thinkings to others. All people annoy him. Thems quiet is too quiet but more bad is when they speak. All things annoy him also. Sun is too hot or too shy, ground too hard or too mush, water too wet.

True is, again since snotnose, everything want to kill him. Snake bites, rat bites, stiffneck disease, newmonia, typho and thick throat have all try to finish him and he have piss on all of them. Diseases he fight. People he do not. He prefer to hear than speak. Watch. Wait. Avoid.

Gommel he cannot avoid. Gommel he cannot offend, cannot say No to. Gommel is high up.

'You think books is bad?' he say.

'Perhap,' say Howul.

'Why?'

'Perhap not then.'

Howul soft mumble so perhap Gommel wont hear. It is no matter. Gommel already know what he will say.

'Everyone here say books kill People Before, isnit?' he say. 'Everyone say they is dangerous. Idiots. What people think and say soon go. What is write down stay.'

Howul nod like so much clever impress him. Gommel use hims stick to lift him out of chair and stand up. Howul go to help him but Gommel tcha him away, hobble two step forward then point back at the chair with stick.

'Move it,' he say.

Howul put the glop and insects book down and try to lift the chair. He cannot. It is heavy as wet sand. As per the usual, he think. Nothing ever easy. He press hims shoulder against it and push. It slow slide across the wood floor and reveal a black mark under it like this –

+

Gommel lean forward and press on the mark with hims stick. A plank lift up. He point at a space under it. Howul kneel down and do as ask even though smell tell him not to. He reach in and touch soft mess. He pull hand out. Gommel hiss and cough. Howul put hims hand back in and this time touch something cold and metal. A red box of People Before about the size of two bricks. He take it out. In its lock is a teeny grey key.

'Open it,' say Gommel.

Howul can hear something inside shake and shuffle. He turn the key. It stick, need oil. Howul know it but still give

Gommel stupid look. In Blanow, stay stupid is stay safe.

Gommel point at a sea shell lamp that rest on a wood stand.

'Pour in some oil, isnit?' he say.

The oil make the box open easy. Inside is a leather pouch the size of Howuls hand. He take it out. All leather is of People Before, brown or black, hard as oak. Alway it smell like stale pattycakes. But this is light blue, soft as baby skin and smell strong of lavender. A metal band seal it. He pull to undo it then stop and look stupid at Gommel again.

'Yes,' say Gommel. 'Open it. It is yours.'

Howul pour what is inside pouch onto hims hand. A sprig of dry lavender, four teeny blood red pencils with black points sharp as needles and four teeny books. He open the page of one book then hold it up so Gommel can see.

'Whats the matter?' Gommel ask him.

'It is blank,' he say loud enough for Gommel to hear easy.

Deep creases run across Gommels face as he hiss cough.

'I learn you to read and write so you can fill it with your words,' Gommel say. 'What hap to you in Blanow. What people say and tell you. Do this and I will make sure things is more good for you here. Books is not dangerous, Howul. People is dangerous.'

Why he choose me? think Howul. Nothing hap to him except avoid everyone.

Gommel point at the lift up plank. Howul push it back in place. Gommel then point at the glop and insects book. As Howul open it, the stink of old mushrooms hit him again.

A boy snotnose sit on soft neat green grass. Hims plumpy face is spit clean. He wave one hand and smile.

Gommel wipe dribble from hims chin and point at the words.

'"My name is Jack," it say.'

Stay stupid, stay safe.

'It is wrong. My name is Howul.'

Hiss. Cough.

\#

After he leave Gommel, Howul take the rocky path that go to Place for Lookout. It cling to the side of the sea cliff and, as you walk, it become more and more steep. Roots of bay tree rip and pull at it but he have use it many time and know just where to place each foot and which way to lean so that he can move fast along without fall.

He like that others cannot easy follow him.

Every day he is here to warn if People Outside approach Blanow. He sit in a grass coom with cliff above and round which protect him from the wind. Today there is no cloud. The sea is slow and half sleep. As they reach the rocks below, each wave is a weak slap. Like a huge vulture, most time the sea rest and do little. But when it wish, it can tear all apart in a flash.

Near him lemon thyme and other sweet scent herbishrubs push through the grass. Flutterbys flit through the air on white or yellow wings. Green, red and black ants crawl round and over hims toesys. Redback lizards scurry over stones and bumblybees buzz and pester every herbishrub they find.

All is keriss and gentle, even for Howul.

Of a sudden he see in the distance some bright yellow oildrums. On them is three People Outside. They have tie themselfs to the sides so they do not roll into the water but now the ropes is loose. All life is beat out of them. As he see Howul, one of them raise slow hims head. Sun have give hims face the colour of pomegranate. Every part of him is scab and scratch and bleed.

He try to stand. The oildrums separate and water wash over them. Pomegranate Face hold onto one. The others fall in water.

Howul go back along the path to the village. He tell Tall Nole to fetch Brenin, Mister Yorath. Soon people gather on the mud shore. Boy snotnoses push forward for a more good look. All watch and wait. Howul is first to see the loose oildrums. Big waves push them more and more close. Pomegranate Face still hold onto one. The other men float face down. Growups move snotnoses away so Mister Yorath can have more good look at where Howul point. Where oildrums is, the sea is fill with monisters. No one go in the water. Everyone wait for the waves to bring everything to them.

Two oildrums is wash in first, then two dead. When they is near as spit, Tall Nole and Droo pull them onto shore. Next is Pomegranate Face. Tall Nole grab him by the arms and lay him down. Hims clothes is rip rags and he do not move. When Tall Nole nudge him with hims foot, he turn over so hims face is in mud. Droo drag other oildrum to shore.

Everyone wait for Brenin Mister Yorath to speak.

'He have weapon?' he ask.

'None I see,' Howul say.

Tall Nole lift him up, wrap hims arms round hims stomach and shake him. No weapon. The shake make Pomegranate Face cough and splutter and gob. He open hims eyes as Tall Nole lay him again on the mud.

'How many more of you is there?' Mister Yorath ask him.

Pomegranate Face lift up hims head and look round like he do not know who say this. Then flop back in the mud without answer.

'Is there any more?' Mister Yorath ask Howul.

'Only them, I think.'

He nod at the two dead skinbones also drag from the sea.

'We will look after you,' Mister Yorath say to Pomegranate Face. 'What is your name?'

Pomegranate Face squeeze hims eyes to rid them of salt then gob out more water.

'What is your name?' Mister Yorath ask him again.

'Barry, son of Tom, son of Shane.'

'How many more boats is there?'

'No more.'

'Where is you from?'

'Hale. Have you water? My throat is dry sand.'

Mister Yorath smile and send Droo to bring water.

'Why you leave Hale?' Mister Yorath ask.

'In Hale, there is six men for every woman,' say Barry.

'You is here to find a woman?'

'Yes.'

'We will find one for you.'

Barry try to stand up. Hims knees give and he sit.

'No hurry,' say Mister Yorath.

Droo give Barry a jug of water. He drink huge gulps. He smile then touch hims mouth in pain as the smile crack open hims sunburn skin. He lean back and pour water over hims face then lean forward and pour over rest of head. As he do this, Tall Nole crash a heavy stone onto hims skull. Water and blood spray from hims mouth as he fall more forward.

Some watch, some look away as Tall Nole bring the stone down again and again. Soon hims head is crush watermelon.

People Outside bring weapons and disease, need food, want women, drink water. This is how Blanow welcome them.

\#

Gommel have two books for Howul. Jack and Julie Learn To Read and The A B C Book. He use them to learn Howul what is letters and words and how to say them and write them. He get Howul to read the words out to him many time and to write them down in other teeny books he give him.

Many is not words Howul ever say nor is write how anyone might say them. Nut is Nut but Nite is Night and Nee is Knee. Neville wear a anorak, eat jelly and go tobogganing. Gommel tell Howul that anorak is hat, jelly is type of fruit and tobogganing is climb tree. Howul want to ask how Gommel know this but listen and wait instead.

People in Blanow like storys. When day is dark and only fire give light, someone tell others of what People Before have do. Story of bad Brenin call Macdeth, of big sea monister call Mobby Dick, of man call Drackiller who bite people till they do what he want. Storys everyone know but is tell in different ways.

Howuls father Garith have tell best storys. Alway he fill them with the bad things people do and what you can do if bad things hap to you. This is not how Jack and Julie Learn To Read nor The A B C Book is. Everyone know that for People Before weather is more cold. But here sun shine alway. No one suffer. All is happy. Billy is happy because Granny give him biscuit, Mary because Uncle Jim show her hims stamps and Dulcie because a jolly sailor smile at her. Biscuit is same as pattycake, say Gommel. Stamps is teeny pictures. Jolly is old. Sailor is man with beard.

All this bore the crap out of Howul. He give up with stay stupid and show he learn quick instead. Gommel want him to learn so he can write what hap to him in Blanow, what people say and tell him. If he can write this for him, perhaps Billy, Mary and Dulcie can all gofuck.

Today he have bring the leather pouch from the red box with him to Place for Lookout. Part of him wish he have not so he have reason not to write anything yet. He look at teeny blank pages in teeny book and every page seem huge. What to put on them? A million different thinkings rush into hims head. Not of what hap now in Blanow but bad things that hap before to him. This he do not want to write.

Till she die in cyclone, Jen have give him eighteen good year. Still he baffle at how she have stay warm to him for so long. Not for hims face which is cod fish ugly as well as grumpscrut. Most think he is mirth and merry as tooth ache. Somehow she see him different. She find sweet where others find sharp. She melt hims freezywater. He wish she melt it still.

Instead of write, he put book away and look out at the sea. Beneath the water, grey shadows slew and shift. One time a mouth the size of a snotnose push up against the surface. A sea monister.

Dark clouds fight with the sun for different pieces of the sky. Waves throw themselfs hard against the rocks far below. Rain now fall on him. Big rain. Soon he is drench.

He remember the books. The rain will have mush them. He do not wish to give mush books back to Gommel. When rain stop, he open the pouch. It is miracle pouch. Wet outside but inside all is still dry.

He pick up the pencil again.

Write what hap to you in Blanow, Gommel have say.

'At this moment I sit and look at weather then scratch itch on my bollocks.'

Why write that? He do not.

Then he think of something else. New. Different. Not just copy from Jack and Julie Learn To Read nor The A B C Book.

Because the book is teeny, every letter he write in it is the size of a ladybird leg. The words please him. Each is straight and true.

It is not all spell as we spell but, at thirty five year, this is what he first write –

A is for
Arseholes
Jack and Julie is Arseholes

B is for
<u>B</u>ig
Jack and Julie is <u>B</u>ig <u>A</u>rseholes

C is for
<u>C</u>ocomber
Jack and Julie can shove <u>C</u>ocombers up thems <u>B</u>ig <u>A</u>rseholes

D is for
<u>D</u>ie
Jack and Julie <u>D</u>ie from shove <u>C</u>ocombers up thems <u>B</u>ig <u>A</u>rseholes

E is for
<u>E</u>veryone
<u>E</u>veryone is please Jack and Julie <u>D</u>ie from shove <u>C</u>ocombers up thems <u>B</u>ig <u>A</u>rseholes

F is for
<u>F</u>ood
<u>E</u>veryone is please Jack and Julie <u>D</u>ie because they waste <u>F</u>ood by shove <u>C</u>ocombers up thems <u>B</u>ig <u>A</u>rseholes

G is for
<u>G</u>ofuck
Jack and Julie can <u>G</u>ofuck with thems spitcleen shiny smily faces, neet hair that never mess, tite clothes that never rip as they play with animals they never kill nor eet, jump in water that never drown them, never have rain nor mud nor syclone nor dark nor hunger nor deth but only cleen noo soft dry plumpy safe
<u>A</u>rseholes

He have make a start. But he decide not to show it to Gommel just yet.

#

Howul wake as the sun first show. Eyes thick with brick dust, he rub right and left with thumb to clear them before open. Hunger is already a big fist inside hims stomach.

The dust and hunger hap every morning so every morning he wake up annoy. He lie still and do as Jen have learn him. He close hims eyes again and try to send hims mind where everything is good. Here he can hold her and feel her soft snores on hims shoulder and smell again the jasmine in her hair. Rain do not fall. Hands do not freeze. Death is not greedy.

He do not lie long before he hear a soft skitter across the floor. With breath hold, he pull away the blankets and pick up the brick he keep close as he sleep. He watch as a rat stop and begin to lick himself. He throw the brick. And miss.

Hims house is one concrete floor, one up wall and three crumple down walls. The cyclone have leave it more down than up. The roof is off, the ceilings is collapse and every weather is let in. Dust from the fall down bricks cover everywhere. If he wish, he can live in the Barn where other men with no women is. He do not wish this. Neither do they.

He stand up and walk over to the rat trap he have set before he sleep. Its lid is drop and the bait is take but inside is empty. As ever.

Every day start the same for him. Hunger, annoy, brick dust, mind walk, empty trap. To help mind walk, he take from under bricks hims keepsakes.

Of hims father Garith, a teeny glass bottle of medicine.

Of hims mother Mags, the feather of a pure white pigeon she have keep and not kill.

Of Jen, hairs from her head he take after she die.

Of hims daughter Erin, a stone she one time say remind her of him. Thin, grey and sharp.

He look careful at each like he have never see them before, blow dust off them, kiss them and put them back under same bricks.

Light now sneak down the tall cliffs behind Blanow. Round them already the red kites and vultures swoop and glide.

He hear a cough. Outside hims house stand Reeta. Small, craxy and scrunchface, she alway have something wrong with her. Back, stomach, legs, head, arms, teeth, heart, kidneys or somewhere she have no name for yet.

As well as most fast, most good eyes and most grumpscrut face, Howul is best go-to person if you is sick.

The wall beside Reeta is fall down. Except for the snake skin in hims hair and bangle of white shells on hims wrist, Howul is total barearse naked. Reeta pretend she do not see him and look at the earth as he wipe crud off hims britches then put them on. He take hims time. Next he pick up leaf shirt, shake it out, put it on. Next, shoes. Shake out, put on, walk, stop, take off, shake out again, put on again.

He step over the wall.

'Oh,' he say. 'I do not see you. How long you stand there?'

'My stomach hurt and I have not shite for three day,' she say.

'You know I have nothing here,' he say. 'Everything to treat you is by The Green.'

'It is emergency. I cannot walk.'

She screw up her face, clutch her stomach and groan.

'Open your mouth big,' he say.

She do so. Her tongue is swellup a little but still a good pink.

'Open your eyes big.'

She do so. They is clear and bright.

'You cannot walk?'

'No.'

'So how you get here?'

She clutch her stomach again to avoid answer. He press it with hims hand in different places and ask her where it hurt. It hurt everywhere.

'You have to wait till your stomach do not hurt,' he say. 'This take time. Lie down on the ground here and do not move till I is back this evening.'

'It is emergency,' she say.

'It is cramp,' he say.

It is neither. It is nothing.

'Till you can walk again, all we can do is wait. Stay here till I return and do not move.'

Every day he tell her to do something she wont want to do. This way he hope she will leave him alone. But next day she is back and ask about something else. Perhap every day she think he heal her.

He leave her and walk down the brown scorch earth path to

where tall cypress trees hide two ponds. He shite in shite pond and wash in wash pond.

He is first here and alone, as he prefer. No one to talk gobbledybollocks to him nor complain about stinks and unclean water as they make stinks and unclean the water.

Next he walk more far down the path to The Green. This is also scorch earth except the small grass mound where only Mister Yorath can stand or sit. As Blanow Brenin, he do not stand nor sit there much as he have so many other important Brenin things to do. Sleep under warm blankets. Eat tinfoods. Have Glend cut hims hair or clean hims toesynails.

Far enough from the grass mound so no ash fall on it, Big Tris mind the fire. Soot is on her forehead. Crumbs is on her chin. Tea brew. Pattycakes cook. Big Tris keep taste them to be sure they is still pattycakes and have not turn into pebbles nor lumps of metal nor tortoises. Most plumpy woman in Blanow, she have most to squeeze and hold and kiss. As men like. Men want her even more than they want her pattycakes.

The Senter is behind The Green. The wood is long since take from its floor but its thick slate walls and roof still easy fight off cyclone. Howuls daughter Erin and the other girl teens sleep here. She cross from it now and wait in line for pattycake. Every day she look more like her mother Jen. Same frizzy black hair, same huge brown eyes that can melt heart and freeze blood in two blinks. Like Jen, her top lip rest on bottom lip like she hide a hazelnut under it. Like Jen, she is dark skin even in white season. Since Jen die he give her any extra food he get but still she become more and more skinbone.

Big Tris tip a pattycake from the hot metal onto her wood plate. Erin move away from the other girl teens and sit by herself under a silverbirch. She lean her thin back against it, put down her plate and place her fingers on her head to check Jens cloth ribbon is still there. The colour of rowan berrys and two fingers wide, it is tie so tight her hair burst out behind like rosemary bush. Howul join her. She groan. He point to the pattycake on the plate beside her.

'Eat it. You is all bone.'

She give him her Your Brain Is Fill With Ash And Shite look.

'You must eat,' he say.

'It taste of grit,' she say. 'You eat it.'

She push the plate toward him. If it stay there the red kites may get it. He pick up the pattycake and bite into it. It taste of grit.

'Chew it careful, isnit?' he say.

'I know how to eat, Dad.'

He put the plate on her lap. She put it on the ground again.

Now Jen is no more, there is only him to look after her.

'Jen want you to eat,' he say.

'You have ask her?' she say.

Two red kites swoop down and snatch the pattycake. He look away so she cannot see how piss off he is with her.

He want to be good father. Before, he leave so much to Jen because Erin seem to need her more. He wish he have do more then so he know what to do now. Everything he try just go pigsarse.

He try to remember how Jen speak to her, how she get Erin to like her, how she get her to do as she ask. Be kind, he think.

'I get my pattycake now,' he say. 'You can have it.'

'Yours is special? Yours have no grit?'

'Please, Erin. You have to eat.'

'I do not have hungry.'

She stand up to walk away from him. He grab her twig thin arm. Where he press stay white like no blood ever reach there.

'Fucksake eat something,' he say.

Her Ash And Shite look fade to deep hurt. Jen never grab her arm.

'Sorry,' he say. 'Sorry.'

She walk away.

On way to Big Tris for pattycake he go past the wood shack where he store oils and medicines. Eddy, Si and hims boy Lorunse wait for him here. Lorunse cry as soon as he see Howul. All snotnoses think he hurt them for fun. He try to walk on but Si stop him and show him six blisters Lorunse have on hims foot where hims bark shoes have rub. All of them is burst.

Howul prefer blisters, boils, sores, wounds, corruptions, diseases to people. He understand them more. To try and heal and mend empty hims mind of all else. He just wish no people is around as he do this.

'Do he scratch the blisters?' ask Howul.

'I tell him not to,' say Si.

Lorunses lips wobble as Howul smear the blisters with elderflower oil. He tell Si to wrap the foot in camomile leafs and keep him away from shite pond. Lorunse scream like Howul have just stab him.

'He like shite pond,' say Si.

'He like shite pond?'

'Yes.'

'That I cannot heal.'

Lorunse wail as Si lead him away.

Eddy have bad abscess on hims arm. He have same year as Howul and work all day with hot metal. He ignore the burns, bleeds and bruises this give him but this abscess is big as hims thumb, oozy and bright red.

Howul get a knife from the shack and put it in the fire where Big Tris is. As he wait for it to heat, he get pattycake from Big Tris.

'You have two? Birds take Erins,' he say.

She tcha.

'You think I is make of pattycake? Others have hungry too.'

He want to save hims for hims daughter but the fist in hims stomach do not let him. He eat it and take the heat knife back to Eddy.

'Bite this,' he say and give him a piece of pinewood.

He use the knife to cut and drain the abscess. Eddy make no fuss.

'Keep it clean with fresh ashes,' Howul tell him.

Eddy nod and hurry away so he can sear and scald himself some more.

Milani now wait for him also. She say she have knee shake. Her left leg is brack bad when she is a snotnose. Howuls father Garith reset it but she never can full straight it. She is still for sure the most keriss woman in Blanow even more than Big Tris. Eyes clear, hair thick and arse like ripe apricots. Hers is the fine, full plumpiness all women want. No women like her. Most men like her too much. She behave like they is all cack. This make them like her more. Most want to dob her. Howul want to dob her now.

'It shake when I squat,' she say.

'You can show me?'

She tcha, make big sigh then squat. Her left knee shake. She stand up. Her knee is good again. Howul do not know why this hap.

'Do not squat,' he tell her.

'How else do I take a shite?'

'Show me again.'

She squat again. Her knee shake again. He hold it and the shake stop. Her skin is soft and she smell of fresh rose petals. He let go.

'You try.'

She hold her knee but still it shake as she squat.

'Hold it more firm.'

She try with no difference. He press her knee here, there, here, there and ask if anything hurt. Nothing hurt. She sniff and move her leg away.

'Can you stop it from shake or no?'

Howul frown at her to show how hard he think.

'Here is what we do,' he say. 'Rest it as much as you can. Also I will make a special potch for you. Eat it and your knee will stop from shake. But it may take longtime, isnit?'

'How long?'

'Less long if you chew every glopful forty time before you swallow.'

'You serious?'

'It give heal the best chance. But it is not heal. It is knee.'

As soon as he say this he wish he have not.

Milani stand up, shake her head and limp away. He watch her go then see Reeta now approach the shack. She hold her stomach and walk slow, as if each step is her last. As she reach Howul, she stagger and sit down.

'You can walk again. Thats good,' he say.

'Today I is too sick to work,' she say.

Work for her is to fetch and carry wood. Alway she want to be ill and stay home. Alway Howul tell her No. He check her tongue and eyes again.

'No,' he say.

She look round to make sure no one see then get out something hide in her skirt. It is wrap in maple leafs. She pass it to him. Inside is a fresh pattycake. She have never do this before. He taste it. No grit. He put it between two hollow out wood slats in hims britches where he can hide what he should not have.

He press her stomach in different places again. She shudder with pain, some time even before he press.

'Go home and rest,' he say. 'I tell Jims you cannot work today.'

As Mister Yorath is oft time so bizzy with eat tinfoods and sleep, Jims look after most things for him. For this he get more food, more blankets, more good house. He think he is important and expect everyone else to think same. Howul think he is arsepain.

'Reeta have bad stomach and cannot work,' he tell him. 'Also I need vegetables for potch for Milani.'

'Reeta some time only pretend to be sick,' say Jims.

'Pretend?' say Howul. 'I must look out for that. But just now it is real. She have not shite for three day. Last shite is soft and still she must big strain to make it. She have try several time since then and nothing come out, neither hard nor soft. Today even when she strain and fart enough to blow down a wall, still she do not shite. She–'

'Okay,' say Jims. 'She can rest. What vegetables you need?'

Jims get Droo to bring him carrots, beetroot, onions, spinach.

So long as no one see, Howul will keep some for himself. Before newmonia finish him, hims father Garith is also go-to for sick people in Blanow. He have many small glass bottles fill with oils from nettle, comfrey, mustard, yarrow, tansy etcetera etcetera. He learn Howul how to make each oil and what to use them for, how to treat bone bracks, how to know from hair, eyes and skin what disease a person have, what is good blood and bad blood. He learn him something else, too.

'To be good go-to, medicine is not enough,' Garith tell him. 'You also need billy bully.'

One time he bring Howul with him to treat Wes, a weak old man with death cough who have not stand nor eat for four day. Garith look in hims eyes and mouth, hold him up and help him walk. Wes do five steps then cough up blood and flem. Garith put him down again so hims skinbone back lean against a wall. Wes chest heave forward as he try to hold back each new cough. He gasp for air.

'You have blight,' say Garith. 'I make a special potch for you.'

'It heal me?' gasp Wes.

'Yes. It heal you,' say Garith.

He say it like he mean it then say it again more loud.

'Most definite it heal you. But you must chew forward then backward every time before you swallow. This will release all the good. And you must chew everything forty time.'

Wes have no teeth and can only drink liquid. Garith pat him on hims arm.

'Together we make you strong again,' he say. 'Potch heal you. Potch heal everything.'

Garith get extra vegetables for Wes and keep some for Mags and Howul. The rest he cook and mash into potch. They take it to Wes. Hims back is still against the wall but now hims chest no more heave. They is too late.

Garith close Wes eyes then share glopfuls of potch with Howul. Both swallow without chew one time, never mind forty. Between them they eat all of it.

'If Wes have get well, everyone think I make miracle. If he die, I tell them it is because he have not chew forty time. No one ever chew forty time,' say Garith.

'What is potch? What is blight?' say Howul.

'Anything you want,' say Garith.

Howul add bitter dandelion leafs to potch he make for Milani. The more bad something taste, the more good people think it do them. He put potch in empty tin and take it to her in the Fields of Flowers. This is where she work. Not by dig potatos, gut fish nor carry wood. Instead she help flowers grow by lie next to them as she sleep or by rub rose petals into her skin.

She sit in the shade of a beech tree, her good leg stretch full out in front of her. She drink mint tea from a wood cup.

'Potch,' he say in case she have forget.

He put it down by her and hope she will ask him to sit with her. She do not. He sit anyway.

'How is your leg now?'

'Fine.'

'Good.'

'Of course it is fine because here I do not squat, isnit?'

'The potch will heal you.'

He hand her the tin. She smell it and pull face.

'Chew every glopful forty time. Forward then backward.'

She put some in her mouth, taste and spit it out. She give the tin back to him. He will eat it all more late on. He do not mind bitter. At least now she cannot blame him if she do not mend.

'I have work,' she say.

How she look, how she smell make him want to stay. He try something else.

'I need your help,' he say.

She edge away a little and flick her hair from her eyes.

'I cannot talk to my daughter,' he tell her. 'I cannot get her to eat.'

'You give her that?'

She point at the potch.

'No. She have same as all. I share all I have and still she eat nothing. Will you talk to her?'

'What for?'

'She have no friends. Other girl teens ignore her.'

'How long she not eat?'

'Since her mother die.'

She sip her tea and brush a midge from her arm.

'Perhap she want to die also,' she say.

He look over at the roses and lillies in the Fields of Flowers. They jostle and fight for every drop of water, every glint of sun, every good they can get from the earth. Red kites fight for every small scrap of food. Sick people he treat fight for thems every last breath. If they can all fight, why wont Erin?

Tears sting hims eyes. He do not want Milani to see this so move away and head along the rocky path to Place for Lookout.

#

Safe in the coom, he hold teeny blood red pencil and stare at blank page in one of the teeny books. If flowers can win thems fight for water and sun, red kites for food, sick people for breath, then least he can do is win fight with blank page.

Ants, lizards, flutterbys, bumblybees all try to lead hims mind away but this time he do not let them. There is much he want to write. He start with Gommel. Pattycakes. Reeta. Potch. It feel good, like he is there again and understand it more. In time he check the sea to make sure no boats approach. He write next of hims father. Milani. Barry. Erin. Jen. Bad things. Hurt. Regret. He wish it is a story he can change.

Then he notice it. A boat of pinewood more big than any he have ever see before.

Oft time four season may pass where no boats arrive. Two in same season is rare.

He count twelve People Outside on it. Three can still move. Two is skullface men with thems hands in the water who try to pull the boat toward the land. Other is a woman with red hair who sit by them and rock back and forward. A long robe stick to her skinbone body like tree sap. The men say something to her and point up to where Howul is.

She try to stand. Her legs shake and she fall back. Her eyes is set so deep in her face it is like she do not have any.

Howul know People Outside bring disease, need food, drink water etcetera etcetera. He know he should go tell the others so Tall Nole can kill them. But the woman have perhaps the same year as Jen when she is first with him. And too near in hims mind still is the smile of Pomegranate Face just before Tall Nole crush hims skull. He do not want to write this of the red hair woman as well. So he wait where he is.

'Help us,' shout one of the men.

'Do not come on shore,' Howul shout back. 'If you land, we kill you.'

He take out the pattycake Reeta have give him and throw it toward the woman. It fall into the sea. She scowl at him. She think he throw a stone at her.

'Keep away,' he shout.

Close to death she watch him as he take from her this last hope.

The waves wash the boat out to sea again. The tide will soon push it toward the mud shore of Blanow. There is no choice for him. He walk back to the village and let Tall Nole know. People gather. Mister Yorath arrive with Jims and Droo. They wait. And wait. No boat.

'Where is it?' ask Mister Yorath.

'Perhap sea monisters have sink it,' say Howul. 'It is more big than other boats. Perhap the tide push it away.'

More wait. More watch. Howul have drag Mister Yorath from tinfoods and warm blankets and still there is no one for Tall Nole to kill. All is disappoint.

'You have waste our time,' say Mister Yorath and go back to Big House.

'You have waste our time,' say Jims who like to repeat what Brenin say.

To tell of the boat is the last thing Howul have want to do. He do it and still is blame. He know this is how life treat him alway but for now he do not care. He prefer blame to more blood spill.

Big Tris is by the fire on The Green. Soot is over her hands, arms, clothes, hair and face. It make her eyes look bright and clear. Smell of cook potatos fill Howuls nose. If he billy bully perhaps she give him more food.

"You have most keriss eyes of all in Blanow," he say.

Hims face is still full grumpscrut so she is not sure if he tease her.

'You have two potatos for me, isnit?'

She shake her head.

'Three?'

With a stick she knock one potato from the fire and push it along the ground toward him. It is most large of those in front of her.

'Others have hungry too,' she say.

He pick it up and wipe off the dirt. Inside is some cook worms, catterpillys and locusts. He throw it from hand to hand as he walk away till it is cool enough to eat. The fire have not reach two of the catterpillys on it. They wriggle and try to scape. He put them in hims mouth and chew.

Erin sit alone by the silverbirch. He go join her. Grass have more flesh on it than do her arms. She have a potato Big Tris have give her.

'I have bad cough and pain in stomach,' she say as reason not eat to it.

He get a small glass bottle of herb oil from hims rocksack and give it to her. She take two small sips then hand it back. Two is more than no. He try to find good father words for her.

'I know you miss Jen,' he say. 'So do I. But she do not want you alway to feel so bad.'

She give him Ash and Shite again.

'I do not want you to feel bad neither,' he say. 'How can I stop it?'

She check Jens ribbon is still in her hair then say –

'Stop treat me like snotnose. Stop bother and pester. Stop tell me what to do. Stop tell me what to eat. Let me be.'

It shock him how much she throw at him, how bad a father he is.

'I worry, isnit,' he say.

'Dont,' she say.

Tall Nole walk toward them and throw her a stupid smile. She drop her head and pretend she have not see him. Though he have only twenty year, already every muscule on him is huge. Like person in story Howuls father have oft time tell, even hims muscules have muscules. He wear People Before pants and no shirt so everyone can see how well rip he is. Hims brains is less develop. They is squish apple.

'What you want?' Howul say.

'To speak to Erin, isnit?' he say.

'She is bizzy.'

He watch her a few moments then say –

'She is not bizzy. She stare at the ground.'

'She think.'

He bend hims knees and smile at her.

'What you think?' he ask her.

Still she stare at the ground.

'She like to be alone when she think,' Howul say.

'I come back when she do not think,' he say.

'Only time she do not think is when she sleep.'

He click hims teeth as he consider this.

'Okay. I come back when she sleep.'

He stand up, scratch hims bollocks and walk away.

'Tell me if he give you any trouble,' Howul say.

'He is piss and wind,' she say.

He wish this is true. Tall Nole is Mister Yoraths bullyboy. What he want he usual get.

Even in this gold season the night cold begin to bite so they go back to the fire. People listen as Garf tell a story. Garfs story is about a boy call Romaro and a girl call Jewel. He love her and pretend not to and she love him and pretend not to. Then they stop from pretend and both die.

Like all storys tell in Blanow, everyone already know it. So the person who tell it add and change what hap in it. This time Jewel cannot see and Romaro cannot hear. Howul wait for Garf to get to where hims story is too shonked for him to fix but Dev and Kirby interrupt him. Dev show him ankle he have twist and Kirby where brambles have cut her face. By the time he have treat them, Erin have disappear and the Garf story have collapse.

'You say Romaro cannot hear but he hear Jewel tell other girl about him,' Martin say. 'You have forget, isnit?'

'I have not forget,' say Garf. 'Love have make him hear again.'

'You do not tell us that before.'

'I tell you now.'

'Because you forget, isnit?'

Howul try to find Milani to ask if she have speak to Erin yet. Both is nowhere so he go back to hims crap house instead. The lid of the rat trap is drop, the bait is take and inside is again empty. He raise the lid and smeer potch as more bait.

The moon throw her strong light into hims house. She show the black burn marks along one wall where People Before have make fires. She show the strange words along another wall write by People Before –

Even Gommel cannot explain them nor other words on walls in Blanow for instance COUNTY P LICE BUILDINGS on The Senter and ICH DIEN on Jerry and Glends house.

'People Before is not like us,' he say.

Even before the cyclone, hims floor carry many loose bricks and slates. As well as keepsakes, he hide other things under them that no one ever find nor steal. This is where he now keep the red box he get from Gommel. He know it is safe because for longtime already he hide here a book hims father Garith have give him.

Hims father is give it by hims father Piter who is give it by hims father Nominus. All have use it to learn the other how to read and write.

Gommel learn Howul what he already know.

Front and back of the book is of thick black leather that smell of stale pattycakes. Between the leather is one hundred and thirty three pages fill with many, many words.

On the first page is this –

A

GUIDE TO HEALTH

BEING AN

EXPOSITION OF THE PRINCIPLES

OF THE

THOMSONIAN SYSTEM OF PRACTICE

AND THEIR

MODE OF APPLICATION

IN THE

CURE OF EVERY FORM OF DISEASE

EMBRACING A CONCISE VIEW OF

THE VARIOUS THEORIES OF ANCIENT AND MODERN PRACTICE

BY BENJAMIN COLBY

Third edition, enlarged and revised

Let us strip our profession of every thing that looks like mystery - RUSH

MILFORD, N.H.
JOHN BURNS

· · · · · · ·

1846

Many of the words in this book is weird but with them it explain how to stop diseases and treat fever, boils, burns, wounds etcetera etcetera. There is pictures in it of plants like Snakeshead, Thoroughwort, Orchid, Lobelia. Much in it he cannot understand but on many pages is extra words Garith, Piter, Nominus and others have add, for instance 'This work good but no one let you do it,' 'Try with honey,' etcetera etcetera.

No one except Erin know Howul have this book.

Gommel is right. Books is not dangerous. Diseases is dangerous. Snakes is dangerous. Rats is dangerous. Water is dangerous. People is dangerous.

He do now as he do at the end of every day. Take the keepsakes from where he hide them under bricks, blow dust off them, kiss them, put them back. Alway so much dust.

Then he think of the pouch. Perhaps there is room in it also for the keepsakes? Keep them clean and dry? He try. There is room. This please him and make him feel clever. He put the pouch back in the red box.

A moment more and he think of the CURE OF EVERY FORM OF DISEASE book. Alway he must blow dust off it also when he take it out from under bricks. Perhaps in red box there is room for it also? To keep it clean and dry? There is room. He feel even more clever. Till he find that, with pouch on top of book, the box no more close. He tcha at how bad world is that do not let clever person like him keep everything in same place. He keep book in box and put pouch under other bricks.

Hims eyes is heavy. He lie on a concrete floor under three leaf blankets and a thick red People Before blanket. They all stink so bad of mildew and old piss that even the rats usual leave them alone.

He pull them over hims head. As he sleep no one in Blanow is sick with stiffneck disease or fever rash. He have no hunger. Jen can hold him, Erin is plumpy and smile at him and, like in Jack and Julie, everything is new and dry and soft.

In sweet dream with mildew blankets over hims head is how he like Blanow best.

#

He hear a noise in the rat trap. After throw off the blankets, he go to it and careful lift the lid. A rat is inside. As he careful lift her out, he see she is pregnens. He push her face to the floor and squeeze her neck till her breath stop. He put her in hims rocksack for Big Tris to add to a scrag soup or stew.

Rats is the enemy so he is glad to catch and kill one. He just wish she is not pregnens.

After shite in shite pond and wash in wash pond, he go to The Green. He is first here. Branches of wood is arrange in five big circles. Within each is black ash and a pigeon with one leg tie to a branch so he cannot fly away. Today there will be Challenge. Someone have die. Others arrive, stand, wait, watch, say little. There is no bustle, no hustle.

Of late there is many deaths and many Challenges. In past eight season, Jen have die in cyclone, Nyra from stiffneck disease, Al from bad brack leg and Andrea, Tam, Kaydor, and Gethin all from big throat disease.

As well as many people die, many people get sick. Five day back Jerry is bite by a rat and now lie abed with yellow skin and red eyes and bleedy nose. Don have sweet piss disease and is now a stink breath skeleton. Fen have one foot swellup to size of a melon, Nance have red eye and Tel cough blood. Gerrun is now blind and deaf and like a baby again.

So who have die? Most like it is Jerry. Or Don. Or Tel. Or Gommel.

Let it be one of them, think Howul.

Already he have lose father Garith, mother Mags, woman Jen and the boy baby who is not let live because only Erin is allow.

'Perhaps she want to die,' Milani have say.

Let me not lose Erin, he think. Let me not lose Erin.

As yet there is no Don nor Jerry nor Tel nor Gerrun nor Gommel. Tall Nole bring a small wood laddyback chair from Big House and place it on the grass mound for Mister Yorath.

Big Tris is by the fire. Howul drop the rat on the ground by her. Blood ooze and drip from the rats eyes.

'I think she like you,' he say.

'How can she? She is dead.'

'Is she? I have not notice.'

She pick up the rat by the tail, drop it into her dead meat sack and give him half a pattycake as reward.

The big front door of Big House is same colour as sky. Everyone is quiet as it open and Mister Yorath make slow ceremony walk to The Green. Hims arms is fold over, chin high and eyes stare only ahead. Jims and Droo walk behind him and behind them is Gommel. Hims stick stab the earth with each wobble step.

At The Green Mister Yorath slow walk to the laddyback chair and slow sit in it. He wear a white cloth shirt, black coat, black britches and black hat of People Before. On hims feet is black leather shoes that keep off dust and thorns. Hims stomach and legs push tight against the sides of the chair.

Tall Nole stand behind Brenin with red kite feathers in hims hand and use them to brush moskits and midges away from him. He also hold up umbrella to keep heat off him.

Alway there is Challenge when someone in Blanow die. The man who win it win the White Dress Woman. This is how Jen become Howuls woman, how Glend become woman of Jerry, how Dee become woman of Si etcetera etcetera. With so many deaths since the last gold season, the only woman who still can be White Dress Woman is Milani. Today they will thread daisys in her hair and she will put on the People Before White Dress. Howul do not know who will win her except not him. Too old, too weak.

Only way to win woman and make child that can live is with Challenge. Some women only ever have women as dobmates. Big Tris and Linda for instance. Some men only dob men. Crayg and Andi. Most men dob men till they win Challenge. Howul have dob Ken and Si and Robut but stop when he win Jen. Since she die he have no dobmate.

Boy snotnoses shuffle thems feet, nudge, giggle and get as close as they can to the ash circles. Women and girl snotnoses swap soft words from behind thems hands so Mister Yorath is not disturb by them. Skeleton Don, cough blood Tel, swellup foot Fen and blind and deaf Gerrun drag themselfs from sick bed to be here.

Don, Tel, Fen, Gerrun and Gommel have not die.

Let me not lose her, think Howul. For all the bad I ever do, food I have steal, lies I have tell, People Outside I have get kill, for all this bad still let me not lose her.

People look over to The Senter where Milani will walk out as White Dress Woman. Those daisys in her hair, that special People Before white dress. They wait. Nothing hap. Now Mister Yorath send Jims to The Senter to end wait. And now Milani walk out with him. Escept she do not have daisys and wear a simple birch skirt. She and Jims pull someone behind them who do not want to follow. Erin. The White Dress swamp her small shoulders and she tread on the front of it as she walk. They pull her by the arms to The Green and put her before Mister Yorath. He smile at her.

Howuls relief that she live give way quick to anger. Usual he do all that is expect of him. When Jims eat whole roast pigeon and Howul starve, he say nothing. When Mister Yorath is in hims Big House out of the sun and Howul burn all day, he say nothing. But rage now grow white hot within him. Hims daughter have just fourteen year.

'This is wrong,' he say. 'She is too young.'

Mister Yorath take a shiny red cloth from hims black coat and wipe hims face. He do not look at Howul and behave as if he hear nothing.

'Today is a sad day and glad day,' he say to everyone. 'Sad because our dear friend Jerry have pass away. Hims is brave fight but in the end he give up hims life so there can be new life in Blanow. This morning Jims and Droo put him in Field of Black where now he is safe and at peace. Let us remember him.'

Howul bow hims head and remember Jerry. A small, gentle man who never billy bully and have time for all.

As they remember him, Glend hit her forehead with the base of her hand and wail. Glend is Jerrys woman and big with pregnens. Whatever she do Glend alway make big show but this time with fair reason.

Jims try to quiet her but Mister Yorath open wide hims arms for her and Tall Nole lead her to him. She kneel before him and he pat her head as she pull at her hair and make more noise of grief. Then Mister Yorath nod at Jims who nod at Droo who move her away.

'Sad and glad day,' say Mister Yorath. 'Sad for us to lose dear Jerry. But glad for Erin. For her is honour to be choose as White Dress Woman. There will be Challenge. Any man for it, let him now walk up.'

Erin look at Howul as if she think he can make this stop. He know what hap in Blanow if you upset or defy Brenin. You drown. You fall from High Rock. You disappear. You die. Already Howul have say she is too young. More from him and next she have no father.

Tall Nole pour water into hims mouth from stone jug. He drink all of it then walk up and step into one circle of branches and ash. The pigeon make big wingflap and loud screetch as it try to get away from him. He grab it and ring its neck. This is how he declare himself for Challenge.

Howul look at others who also might declare – Ken, Robut, Gav, Lee, Carl, Martin. No one move. All know Tall Nole is more strong than them. Everything in Blanow is now brack. Jen is dead. Erin do not eat and every breath she take is poison to her. If she become Tall Noles woman, it is more bad than if she never have life. Still no one walk forward.

He have fail her as a father. There is no way to save her now but he want her to know he try. Hims mouth taste of smoke as he step more near to Mister Yorath.

'My daughter is too young for this. Milani should be White Dress Woman,' he say.

Jims get Droo to push him back.

'Anyone else for Challenge?' say Mister Yorath.

'Anyone else?' say Jims.

No one move. Then Howul walk over to another ash circle and step inside.

'What you do, Howul?' say Mister Yorath.

'I is for Challenge,' he say.

Mister Yoraths face go the colour of ripe persimmon.

'Step out of circle,' he say.

'Erin is too young. This must be stop.'

No one say this to Mister Yorath. He decide and others do. There is shock breaths and tchas.

'Point of Challenge is to make new life,' Mister Yorath say. 'She is your daughter. You make new life with her?'

'No.'

'Step out of circle.'

'Make Milani White Dress Woman. Then I step out.'

Howul wait. No one say anything. No one move. He take the pigeon in hims hands. It wriggle and flap as he pull hard on the neck and its beady red eyes close. Mister Yorath

38

whisper something to Jims who whisper to Droo. Droo help Mister Yorath out of the laddyback chair and walk with him and Gommel back to Big House. Jims wait till they is away then say to Howul –

'You cannot win. Tall Nole is more strong than you. You hurt you and your daughter. Step out now.'

He smile and offer hims hand. Howul do not take it. The smile die.

'If you have not leave when Mister Yorath return, you is deadman,' he say.

He go to Big House. Everyone else stay on The Green and wait. They look at Howul like only reason he declare for Challenge is to make them stand in sun too long.

Glend move from grief for Jerry to rage at him, as if he have kill Jerry himself. She get as close to circle as she can and shout each word one at a time through sobs –

'I. Hope. You. Is. Please. With. Self.'

She then collapse on ground and wail.

'All of you know this is wrong,' say Howul. 'Why is Milani not White Dress Woman?'

With some struggle, Si and Dee help Glend onto her feet and hold her up. She lean back and fold her arms above her pregnens stomach.

'Mister Yorath know what is best,' she say. 'I lose my Jerry and now you burn us under most brute sun.'

'She is my daughter,' say Howul.

Erins shoulders rise and fall but she keep all sobs inside her. Milani watch over her as if at any moment she will run away in a dress too long for her to walk in.

'You think Mister Yorath is shiteforbrain?' say Tall Nole.

'How old is you when you is White Dress Woman?' Howul ask Hol.

'Twenty,' she say.

'And you?' to May.

'Twenty two,' she say.

'You?' to Glend.

'You is Brenin now?' she say.

'Mister Yorath tell us Fee is too young,' Howul say. 'Erin is more young than Fee.'

Fee have only sixteen year when she get pregnens last white season. She never say who the father is. Mister Yorath tell everyone she is too young to have child. No one see her again.

'If Fee is too young, so is my daughter.'

'Fee is slut. Fee is not White Dress Woman,' say Glend.

Big sky blue front door of Big House open. Mister Yorath walk from it back to The Green with stiff shoulders and head bow forward. Jims and Droo follow with Gommel behind. Mister Yorath get to the laddyback chair, stand by it and wipe hims face with red cloth.

All is still. All watch.

Mister Yorath speak but do not look at Howul.

'You have defy me,' he say. 'That is not allow.'

Howul know he cannot go back. So he go forward instead.

'Challenge is wrong,' he say. 'Call it off.'

'Challenge is Challenge. No sick in mind person can change that,' say Mister Yorath.

'He call you Shiteforbrain,' say Tall Nole. 'He should be disqualify.'

'Last time. Step out,' say Mister Yorath.

'Not till Challenge is call off.'

Mister Yorath take off hims People Before black hat, fan himself with it and put it back on. He show everyone how careful he consider what to do. But all is decide already. He nod to Jims who get Droo to go over to the other circles and loose the strings of the pigeons in them. The birds step careful away like they do not want anyone to notice them and tie them up again. Then they make big wingflap and fly off.

Mister Yorath take off hims hat again and wave it up and down three time.

'Challenge is now begin,' he say.

He walk slow back to Big House.

Droo pick up the laddyback chair and follow.

'Challenge is now begin,' say Jims.

Milani pull Erin by her wrists back to The Senter. Big Tris stoke up the fire and put pattycakes onto it. Tall Nole and Howul stay in thems circles.

When he have win Jen in Challenge, Howul is young and strong and know he have more stay than others. Also before it he have drink many jugs of water. He still have more stay than most in Blanow but hims head is already hot bricks and hims throat sand. Flies already buzz round hims dead pigeon.

Everyone else go to do thems work. Si to throw hook lines

and nets into the sea, Robut to pull them out with any fish they catch. Eddy to use fire to make metals soft and to beat them into new shapes. Fred and Andi to dig in Big Fields while Gale pull out weeds and Nic wave hims arms to keep birds away. Reeta to carry wood. Girl teens to make barley dust into pattycakes for Big Tris to cook. Harol to pump water from the well and boy teens to take it in buckets to anyone who need. Kim and Crayg to keep the chickens safe and bring in eggs.

Without Howul, Ken and Treva go to Place for Lookout instead. Thems eyes is not as good as hims so there is two of them for watch.

Howul pick up the dead pigeon, pull back hims feathers and use a stone to separate skin from meat. He drink the blood and chew on dark pink flesh. Tall Nole shout at him.

'Soon I have your daughter,' he say.

'You cannot win,' say Howul. 'I learn myself not to need water. You have learn that?'

'Here is my water,' Tall Nole say and piss on the ground.

Howul turn hims back to him, close hims eyes and mind walk to Nobody Beach.

Most time a thick wall of cliff stop you from get there but when the water is far enough back you can go round to it from the mud shore. When first he is with Jen, they like to be there alone. They lie on grey slates as he touch her hair and kiss her shoulders and neck.

Nole shout more things as flies buzz round Howuls face. He do more of what Jen have learn him. He sit still with cross legs, breathe slow in and out and try to go where nothing will reach him. Where sweet lemon thyme grow at Place for Lookout. Glossy, pale green leafs. Small, lilac flowers that hide but have a scent so strong that even the most lazy bumblybee still make hims way toward them. He smell the scent. For Jen. For Erin.

Next he look out at the sea and study the different pattern each wave make. Some rise more high than they should and splash big when they fall. Tall Nole waves. Some is wide and slow and you watch every curve and swell. Mister Yorath waves. Some never go where you expect them to. Erin waves. Some is angry, hard to stop and oft time disappoint. Howul waves.

The sea is all deep blue till you look more close. Then you notice the grey black where the sharp rocks and People Before metal is just below the top and the dark black where the water drop down as deep as any cliffs reach up.

He watch the vultures as they circle round the tops of the cliffs. Quick, slow, high, low, close then far apart for so long without rest nor stop.

Waves, vultures, sweet lemon thyme. All help block bad thinkings. But still time pass slow and burn of sun torment him. Then, of a sudden, the vultures shift and fly away from the cliffs and out over the water. In the distance he see a big pinewood boat. The birds swoop down and drop delicate onto it. Other vultures is there already and hiss and screech at them.

Soon Ken and Treva return from Place for Lookout. People rush to mud shore, see the boat and watch as it get more close. It is the same boat as Howul have tell them of before. This time the tide wash it in to them.

When it is close, Droo, Ken, Treva and others put rope on it and pull it onto the mud. Where before is People Outside is now only rip flesh. The other vultures have already feast several day. Ken climb up on boat and wave hims arms at them. They squeak, screech, hiss, cackle and fly off.

The boat is soon brack up and the wood from it is leave to dry on shore. What remain of People Outside is throw into the sea.

Howul blame himself for not do more to help the red hair woman. He try to hear bumblybees and smell lemon thyme but see instead how she scowl and think he throw stone at her.

It grow dark. People stop work and line up for pattycakes and potatos. The fire throw its light over the men in the two circles but no one pay them much mind. There is little to see till one of them go mad or die or give up and leave circle. But then Glend come over to them. She have no more pregnens and carry her new baby in a shawl of grass and leafs. She hurry between the circles and hold him up so they can both admire him.

A sleepy, dribble mouth, pink face boy with purple birth stain over most of hims back and neck. She hold him close to her and pinch hims nose.

'This is Murf,' she say. 'He look like Jerry.'

He do not look like Jerry, think Howul. Jerry never have frog face.

Some day Jims and Droo will take Murf from her because she already have Rooth. They will take him from her and put him in Field of Black. Perhap soon. Perhap after a season or two. Then no one will see Murf again.

Fill with Murf love and Jerry loss, Glend want others to see her frog face baby. Even a soon for death, bad smell man like Howul who may not givashite. But Howul remember how Jen is with Idris, thems son who is put in Field of Black because already they have Erin. How much they have both love him, how brack they is to lose him.

'You is right,' he say. 'He look just like Jerry.'

Brave sad happy Glend leave.

It start to rain. Howul catch some water in hims mouth and use hims leaf shirt to catch more. Tall Nole groan loud as he try and fail to take a shite. All hims muscules strain but nothing hap.

'Give up,' Howul say. 'You will not win.'

'Soon you is dead and I fuck your daughter up the arse,' Nole say.

The rain stop and, not long after, a girl teen approach. Erin. Still in the White Dress.

She keep her hands above her so anyone can see she do not give anything to her father. She step to the edge of hims circle.

'You look cack,' she say.

'Inside I is good,' he say.

She lean forward and talk more quiet so Tall Nole do not hear.

'You must give up,' she say.

'I is still strong. I will win.'

'Accept. I have accept.'

'What have you accept? Tall Nole?'

Her eyes is wet. When she wipe them, her dusty hands make more tears. She blow her nose on the White Dress.

'I will win,' he say.

He know she do not believe him. Tall Nole now crouch with hims knees apart. He do not want Erin to see nor hear it, but again he try to shite.

'I will win this else I is not your father.'

She now talk so soft that Howul have to hold hims breath to hear.

'Milani speak to me.'

'What she say?'

'Gobbledybollocks about mum. Dont wimp, get over, move on. Then she tell me that for you to win is not possible. Everything is fix.'

'Nothing can stop me. I will save you.'

'You cannot save me. Stop. Give up.'

'No. You will see. I will win.'

He say it to keep them both strong but if she stay more time he is disqualify. She blow him a kiss and walk away.

Everything is fix, she say. How? He think if he stay wake, perhap he find out. The fire is out and clouds now hide the stars and moon. He walk round circle or crouch on ground to make sleep more hard. He dig fingernails into hims skin, rub ash into hims eyes but still they is more and more heavy. Some time Tall Nole wake up and groan then go sleep again. Howul scratch hims wrists with stones. Still hims eyes want to close. He rub more ash into them. It sting like fuckery but make no difference. Hims eyes close. He drop off.

A voice wake him.

'Howul?'

He open hims eyes enough to peep through them. The clouds have clear and moonlight wash the ground with grey.

'Howul? You all right?'

It is Jims. He stand near and look him over. Howul do not move. Jims wait.

'Howul?' he say again.

He think Howul sleep. Droo is with him and they tread soft over to where Nole is. Droo go into hims circle and give him gentle kick. Nole splutter and wake. Through the grey light Howul see Droo pass some food and water to Nole.

He close hims eyes as Jims and Droo walk past again.

'Howul?' say Jims.

He stay still. Jims and Droo move on.

With this cheat he know what Erin say is true. It is why Mister Yorath have let Challenge proceed. From the start, Howul have no chance.

There is no ash in hims eyes and hims wrists no longer bleed. But can he now sleep? Can he fuckbuggery.

#

Thirst. Heat. Flies. Putrify pigeon. Cramp in stomach. Piss thick as honey. Bumblybees. Lilac. Lemon thyme.

He do not know nor care what A or B or C or D or E or F is for. If Jack and Julie is here now, he will eat them.

He see Erin walk slow toward him with head low. One of her legs is stiff and cripple and the White Dress is smear with blood. She turn her face to him. A red kite have peck at it and blood pour from wound. She beg him to help but he cannot leave the circle. She fall on the ground.

'You have blight,' he say.

Someone else approach them. It is the red hair woman on the big boat of pinewood that he have tell not to land. Her ribs is even more sharp and her stomach even more hollow than Erins. She walk into hims circle. He try to push her out again but as he do this hundreds of redback lizards climb out of her mouth. He scream with all hims breath. The noise he make bring him out of hims hallooshanins. He is right at the edge of the circle. One more step and he is disqualify.

Every part of hims body now hurt. Hims skin all over is blue and purple.

'You is finish,' say Nole.

Noles skin is clear and clean. Droo must have give him oil for it.

'I is just start,' Howul say. 'I have do all this before. I have win Challenge before. When your skin is on fire and all your body hurt and your throat is swellup and you can no more swallow, still I is here and still I is just start. Give up.'

He wait about ten second then say it again –

'Give up.'

Ten second and he say it again. And again. And again. He wait more long so Nole think he will not say it again then say it again. And again. Only thing that stop him say it more is the dry of hims mouth.

Most time a man win Challenge because others give up. Some time because others die. Nole will not die nor give up. For Howul, it is like try to stop soonarmy with feather.

When it is dark Jims call out Howuls name again and Droo give more food and water to Nole. Howul know he will not last another day.

#

Two boy snotnoses wake Howul up with shouts. He open hims eyes to see Bob, son of Si and Hol, and Nic, son of Colin and Nina, stand as close to him as they can without come into the circle. Both have seven year. In thems hands is clodges and small pieces of slate. They begin to throw them. No growups stop them. Howul smile at them and speak in soft whisper till they stop throw and listen. Howul point to bone and feathers that use to be pigeon.

'When I is out of here I will have hungry, isnit? First thing I do is grab a boy snotnose. Then I rip hims arms off and make him watch me as I eat them.'

As he step toward them, they scream and run away. And now the pain catch him. He clutch hims chest, fall forward, roll onto hims back and struggle to get breath. Hims eyes close and he start to shake. Others hurry over to see what hap. Unless Mister Yorath tell them to, they cannot come into the circle to help.

'He is try to say something,' say Glend.

Howul start to get up but hims arms and legs shake too much for this. Glend scream as he fall back and lie still. Year seem to pass.

There is big murmur of voices and excite whispers. Then all go quiet as Mister Yorath arrive.

'He is dead,' say Glend. 'Nole have win.'

'This is what hap to people who do wrong,' say Mister Yorath.

A go-to should now walk into the circle and care for Howul. Only go-tos that remain is Timmo and Pat. Both is somewhere else.

Another year seem to pass.

Nic throw another clodge at Howul. It stick to side of hims face. He do not move. Other snotnose throw more clodges.

'He is dead,' say Glend again.

Many cheer. It serve Howul right. Tall Nole move from hims circle to The Green. Big Tris give him pattycake.

Then, after another year, billy bully end. Howul open hims eyes and stand up. No shakes, no collapse.

'Nole leave circle,' he say. 'I win.'

After stand up too quick, hims legs fill with concrete and

he fall on hims knees.

'You cheat,' say Tall Nole.

'Tall Nole win,' say Mister Yorath.

'Tall Nole win,' say Jims.

Jims and Droo go into the circle and grab Howuls arms. Dark fill hims brain as they drag him away.

When he come to, he is on lush green grass in front of Big House. Every window of it have unbrack glass and black cloths behind that shine like magpie wings. He is never so close to it before.

Two steps lead up to the big sky blue front door. It is make of metal and stick on it is a strange animal face inside a gold circle. Feet pass him and go up the steps. He look up. Mister Yorath.

'Come,' he say.

Howul look round to check he mean him. Stay stupid stay safe, though perhaps too late for that. He stand up and follow Mister Yorath inside. Lily flowers and apples share thems scent with him so that inside smell like best of outside.

A metal spiders web hang down from the high ceiling. Mister Yorath clap hims hands. Round pieces of glass on the spiders web throw out bright yellow light.

Before Howul is a room four time as big as all hims house. Throw a clodge of earth and it will not reach the wall on the far side. That wall is white as new snow. In the middle of the room is a heavy wood table with wood chairs round it enough for twenty people. The floor is wood also. Unlike other Blanow homes, no one take wood from here to burn or build with.

'Follow me,' say Mister Yorath.

What else is Howul to do? If Mister Yorath want him dead, he is dead already. They walk round the table and over to a wood door. This lead into a room only the size of Howuls house. The table in it have only four chairs round it. Thems seats is of green leather so shiny it is like no one have ever sit on them. On the walls is pictures of People Before with fierce faces and grey hair like baby pigeon feathers. Thems bodys is cover over with more clothes than even Mister Yorath wear. Again there is light in this room from a high spiders web.

'Sit down,' say Mister Yorath.

Howul do so. The chair creek and shake as if angry with him.

He do not know why he is here nor what will hap. But in Big House the man Mister Yorath usual is have go somewhere else. He smile at Howul and pick up jug of water on table. He pour some into a piece of thin glass shape like a tulip head.

'Drink,' he say.

Why have he not just give Howul the jug to drink from? Howul drink and soon the glass is empty. He have not drink anything except rain water for several day. Mister Yorath pour out more water. Howul drink it. Pour. Drink. Pour. Drink. Still Mister Yorath smile as if to watch Howul drink is most good way to spend time..

Next he put on the table People Before plates, dishes and spoons, same as Gommel have.

'Glencare, lumbardo and wedjwoo,' he say.

Howul nod hims head as if what he hear is not gobbledybollocks to him. The plates have on them white flowers and bright skys. The dishes have on them blue birds. The spoons is of metal with no rust.

Mister Yorath go over to a white box as tall as himself and even more wide. When he open it, a big hum start up. The white box is cram with meat, pattycakes, bottles, jugs and many tinfoods. He bring Howul from it a pattycake and another jug of water. This time, he let Howul pour out the water himself. The pattycake taste of honey and lemon. The water is cold as a winter stream.

Tinfoods. Everyone in Blanow know of them but few eat them. They is not like other Blanow foods and do not smell bad if you open after keep for longtime. People Before have make them and still now you can eat them without vom or die.

Gommel eat them. Some time when Gommel sleep Howul taste what is leave. The sweet is more sweet, the salt is more salt than any other food he eat.

Mister Yorath jab a sharp piece of metal into a tinfood, work it round in a circle and take off the top. Inside is big red lumps that he pour into Howuls dish.

'Eat.'

They is the most sweet and most salt big red lumps Howul have ever taste.

'Tomato,' say Mister Yorath.

'Tomato?'

'Yes.'

'Because it is red?'

'Not because it is red. Because it is tomato, isnit?'

For a moment the outside Mister Yorath return. Howul have offend hims tinfoods.

'Tasty,' Howul say.

Mister Yorath smile and open another tinfood fill with small brown lumps and big pink lumps. He pour them onto Howuls plate. They is the most sweet and most salt brown lumps and pink lumps Howul have ever taste. More tinfoods is open and bring to him. One look like grit and dirty teeth.

'Lentools,' say Mister Yorath.

One look like thin worms.

'Spagitty.'

One look like carrots.

'Carrots.'

'My stomach is fill up,' Howul say.

Mister Yoraths smile freeze.

'But it is so tasty I have to eat more.'

Mister Yorath pour out some white liquid

'The more white it is, the more good. This is best of best of best. Condense milk. You is lucky man, Howul.'

Howul taste it and feel sick. He never before eat anything so sweet.

Mister Yorath point to a picture on the wall of a old man with cold eyes and hair as big as a vulture.

'You know who he is?' he say.

'One of People Before.'

'Yes. But who?'

'I dont know any People Before.'

'Hims name is Cadogan. A brave soldier.'

He want me to givashite, think Howul. Pretend you is interest.

'What hap to hims hair?' he say.

'People Before do many things different.'

Still Howul try to work out how best to behave with him. People who defy or upset him alway die. Already Howul have defy and upset him. But Mister Yorath treat him now as if he is hims son or best friend. He stand up and walk over to the white box again. He return with three bottles with words on them Howul do not know. What is Brewery? What is

Wadworth? What is Devizes?

'What is?' he say.

'Beer, isnit,' say Mister Yorath. 'It is drink.'

'And why do the white box hum?'

'You have good brain. You watch. You notice. It is fridge. The hum is electrics and make everything cold. Try.'

He use different piece of metal to take top off bottle and hand it to Howul.

It taste like stale pattycakes. Howul burp and sneeze both at same time. Mister Yorath laugh but hims eyes is cold and dead. Like Cadogan.

Mister Yorath drink from bottle. In a few mouths he finish all of it. He suck back a burp and open another bottle.

'People say you is clever. That is why I get Gommel to learn you to read and write. You like to read and write?'

No one in Blanow read and write. Books is dangerous. Howul say nothing.

'You think books is dangerous?' say Mister Yorath.

Still he say nothing.

'Books is books. Books do not kill people. You know anyone is kill by a book? Books do not kill People Before. People Before kill–'

He stop to speak as another burp try to push through. This time he let it out.

'–People Before.'

He smile and wipe hims mouth with hims hand. He show Howul he is same as other Blanow men. He is Brenin, have Big House, eat tinfoods, do little but, like other Blanow men, he burp. No need for Howul to fear him.

'I ask Gommel to learn you,' he say. 'He tell me he have give you books to write in. What have you write in them?'

Howul cough and sneeze again, this time from surprise. So this is why he still live. Mister Yorath and Gommel want the teeny books and what he have write in them back. Gommel have ask him to write what hap in Blanow and what people say and tell him.

'I have write in them what hap in Blanow and what people say and tell me,' he say.

Mister Yorath drink down more beer and let out another burp.

'Where is the books?' he say.

As soon as Mister Yorath have them, Howul is surely finish. But he have to say something.

'I have them in different places. Safe and well hide.'

Warm, relax Mister Yorath do not seem to want to go find them with him now.

'You have write about people in Blanow in them?' he say.

'Many, many words, yes.'

'What you write of Jims?'

Jims is cack and slime. Everyone know this. But tinfoods is vile also and Mister Yorath still want him to like them.

'Jims? Jims is good people,' Howul say.

'Big Tris?'

Big Tris is shiteforbrain greedygus food thief.

'Also good people.'

Mister Yorath smile cold smile, finish beer and get a tall glass bottle from by the tinfoods. On it in big letters it say Bells. Inside is liquid the colour of ginger tea.

He pour some into each tulip glass.

'Try it,' he say.

Howul drink. Flames fill hims throat. He choke and cough. Poison.

He must have give Mister Yorath a wrong answer. But what should he have say? The poison burn deep into him. Soon he will die. It is too late for him to say the right thing even if he know what it is. He do not care. As everything is already brack for him, death is no big matter.

Brenin now drink from hims glass same liquid as Howul have drink. For him there is no choke and cough, only swallow and smack lips.

Howuls face have become hot. Blood push hard against hims skin. Perhaps Mister Yorath have train himself so poison do not kill him.

'You say Jims and Tris is good people,' say Mister Yorath. 'We both know that is not so, isnit? Jims is fickle snake who will eat hims own shite if he think it will get him something he want. Big Tris steal food from snotnoses while everyone else go hungry. So, tell me – what really go on here?'

Howul is confuse. If Mister Yorath want answer to this, why not wait for it before he use poison? If Howul die, how can he tell him or show where books is?

Hims stomach move one way, the room move another.

Hims mind is fog then clear, fog then clear. Hims mouth start to say things before hims brain can stop it. No matter. With only moments to live, he have nothing to lose. He might as well say what is true.

'Of course Jims is fickle snake. Of course Tris steal. But both is nothing compare with Tall Nole. Most evil, dangerous, shooky scumbag in all Blanow, isnit? When anything bad hap here, alway it is him.'

'Like when?'

Howul is confuse again. Mister Yorath already know the bad things Tall Nole do because Mister Yorath ask him to do them. Tall Nole is Mister Yoraths headcrusher.

'It is all in what I have write,' Howul say.

If he try to say more, he think he will vom. To stop the room from spin, he stare at a picture of a red face man with grey rats for hair.

Mister Yorath get another bottle with more strange words on it. He pour some light brown liquid into hims and Howuls glass. Well, why not, think Howul. I will die soon anyway.

He drink. It taste of most sweet oranges.

Mister Yoraths smile creep Howul so he look at picture again.

'What do you wish is different in Blanow?' say Mister Yorath.

He pour more liquid. Howuls tongue is now too big for hims mouth but still he drink.

'I wish Tall Nole is dead,' he say. 'I wish Erin is not White Dress Woman. I wish Milani is White Dress Woman. I wish Milani is my woman. I wish the last day is not hap.'

'I know you is good man who love hims daughter,' Mister Yorath say. 'Alway I try to make this place good place for everyone. You also want Blanow to be a good place for everyone, isnit?'

Howuls face now bleed water. He try to say something and hiccup instead.

Mister Yorath rub hims nose then fold hims hands in front of him on table. He smile dead smile.

'You will have Milani,' he say. 'She will be your woman. I promise. There will be a good house for you. Jerry and Glends house. Your daughter will not be White Dress Woman again till she is ready. Whatever you want you will have. For this, just tell me what people here do that you do not like. Tell me what must end so we can make it good place.'

Howul begin to speak then stop as hims mouth fill with vom. He swallow it.

'You want more?'

Mister Yorath hold up Bells bottle again. Howul groan and shake hims head. He is more confuse than ever. Why have Brenin poison him if he want long talk? He cannot remember what he have already think or say. All he know is that no one can feel this sick and not die.

'So. What is bad in Blanow, Howul? What must change? What must be stop?'

All is clear now. These, Howul think, is my last words. Make them strong. Make them true.

'You,' he say. 'You must be stop. You make Erin White Dress Woman. You give her to Tall Nole. You is more cack and slime than Jims, more thief than Big Tris. Tall Nole is not most shooky scumbag in Blanow. You is. You is cunt, isnit?'

Smile freeze. Face of Brenin return. He tcha, pick up bottle, stand up, leave.

Howul close hims eyes but still the room spin. Vom push up from hims stomach. He stagger over to the tall white box, open it and spill hims guts over everything inside. He wipe hims mouth and go sit down and wait for death.

#

Hims head ache. Hims back hurt. Hims breath stink. A hand inside hims stomach punch and squeeze it. He wish he is dead but is not.

He hear footsteps as someone soft tiptoesy through the big room behind him. He open the door just as the front door close. The scent of fresh rose petals drive out all others. Milani. He understand now why she is never White Dress Woman. She and Mister Yorath is dobmates.

He seem to have survive poison but to live through this day is more than any snake bite, rat attack, stiffneck disease, newmonia, typho or thick throat disease that he piss on before. He have nothing, no one to help him, no place to scape to.

He look again at the pictures on the wall. One plumpy grey face man with a white cloth round each wrist sit on a red chair with a huge book in hims hand. Books is not dangerous? This one is. Throw it well and a rat die.

He hear the front door open again and footsteps approach. Mister Yorath walk into the room with Tall Nole and Droo. He wear a long black robe with a white shirt under it and round hims stomach a red belt. On hims head is a three point red hat. This mean only one thing.

'Move,' he say.

Howul stand up with bricks inside hims head. He lean forward and put hims hands on the table to steady himself. Tall Nole jab him in the kidneys to move him into the big room and over to and out of front door. The sunlight is hot water in Howuls eyes. Tall Nole keep push and prod till they get to The Green. Here everyone wait for them. The laddyback chair is on the mound with two white plastychairs nearby and ash on the ground. Someone is on trial. Howul.

He have defy Mister Yorath, call him cunt. If instead he have say what fine Brenin he is, how well he look after everyone in Blanow, is he now free? If he have let Tall Nole have Erin, is Milani now hims woman? If he have tell of bad things others do, who steal eggs, who steal fish, who steal vegetables etcetera etcetera, is only they on trial? No. Same result for him and they is all in trouble, too.

Mister Yorath sit on the laddyback chair. Tall Nole kick the back of Howuls legs so he fall on hims knees. He tie Howuls hands behind him with rope then push hims head down till hims face is in the scorch earth.

'You know why you must be before us today?' say Mister Yorath.

'To make me Brenin?'

Ash fill hims nose as he say it and most like no one can hear it but it feel good still to defy. He hear footsteps and the sound of other chairs as they is push back and other two people sit. Hims other judges. Gommel and Jims.

'You have disrespect Mister Yorath and bring shame on yourself.'

It is Jims voice.

'Mister Yorath make Blanow a good place for everyone and you want to destroy that.'

'The way you behave toward your daughter is sick and wrong,' say Mister Yorath.

No one shout out to disagree. Howul try to speak but Tall Nole push hims head more into the scorch earth to stop him.

'When someone do wrong, some time we forgive,' say Mister Yorath. 'What Howul do is so bad there can be no forgive.'

Murmurs and mutters show all accept.

'Why is Blanow a good place?' say Mister Yorath. 'Because we is fair and just. If anyone do as bad as Howul do, they must be punish. But because we is fair and just, first we let him speak. This is your chance, Howul. Tell us how sorry you is for all the bad you do.'

Tall Nole loose hims grip and lift up Howuls head with one hand so he can speak. Say sorry, thank Mister Yorath and perhaps there is less hurt. Fast not slow death. But all else is already take from him. All leave to him is to defy.

'Everyone know Erin is too young for Challenge,' he say. 'I do nothing bad. All I do is protect my daughter.'

Tall Nole push Howuls face hard into the earth again.

'You do not protect her, you hurt her,' say Mister Yorath. 'You want her to be your woman. That is not how to protect her. And that is not all. You try to win Challenge by cheat. Still that is not all. We all know books is dangerous but you have learn yourself to read them. Howul read books. You read books, isnit?'

There is gaspings and oooings

He try to say that Gommel learn him but Tall Nole stop him by keep hims face in the earth.

'You is not fit to be here. You will leave straightway and never return,' say Mister Yorath.

Tall Nole lift him up on hims feet and hold hims arms tight behind. Glend tcha and fan herself and baby Murf with pigeon feathers. Milani brush moskits and midges away from her arm. Jims shuffle in hims white plastychair as hims arse overheat. Hims face, all faces is puff with hate toward Howul. If Erin is here, he do not see her.

'Howul is no more,' say Mister Yorath. 'There is no Howul. Now let us work.'

He get up from the laddyback chair and walk back slow toward Big House. Si and Robut throw hate names at Howul as they go to fish. Fred and Andi spit at him then head for the Big Fields. Nic, Bob and other snotnoses throw clodges at him again. Well, at least he make them happy.

Erin is Tall Noles woman. The only way anyone leave Blanow is by drown in sea or drop off High Rock. The only way to leave is to die.

Tall Nole crash a stone hard against back of hims head.

#

Drips of water echo in hims ears. The bricks in hims head is now make of heavy iron. He can smell moss and piss and stale water. He can see nothing. He lie on wet stone and hear the scurry of cockroaches. When he try to stand up he smack hims head against rock. He use hims hands and feet to feel where he is – a narrow cave not much more big than himself. At one end is rock, at the other solid wood. He lean hims head against the wood. Slow death, not quick death.

If he have hims time again, what will he do different? Life in Blanow is about what hap to you, not what you do. Cyclones, snakes, diseases, people who is above you who decide all for you. Should he have accept less, fight more? Say more, do more, change more? He remember where this get him in past few day. He try to be more good father for Erin, keep her from Tall Nole, stop Challenge, save Red Hair woman. And this is where he is now.

Of a sudden, the wood is push back against him. It is a door and someone try to open it. He hear the voice of Gommel.

'You have get yourself in a right pigsarse,' he say. 'We must be quick.'

Howul slide back so Gommel can push it more open. He then crawl out. Moonlight and stars share thems shine with him and show him where he is. The cave is at the foot of the big grey cliffs behind Gommels house. Gommel push the stick he walk with into part of the door and close it. Branches drop down and hide it again.

'What now?' ask Howul.

'Do everything I say, else we both die. Do not speak.'

He lead Howul away from the village and through silverbirch trees that gleam like ghosts and tremble as they brush past them. They walk slow and stop oft time so Gommel can get more breath. They reach a thick wall of holly. Gommel push the stick into it. This open another wood door. They go through and the wall of holly close behind them. A gentle slope take them up over dry earth and rocks to a house Howul know well. A crap house. Howuls crap house.

'I need back what I give you,' whisper Gommel. 'Where is it?'

First Mister Yorath, now Gommel. Both want the teeny books fill with what he have tell about Blanow. They do not kill him till they get them back.

Gommel catch hims breath and wait as Howul go inside. The red box no more have teeny books nor pencils inside it. They is with keepsakes in pouch under others bricks. He fetch pouch and shove it between the wood slats in hims britches. Safe.

He bring the red box to Gommel.

'Here,' he say.

Gommel take it and can feel something move inside it. He do not know it is the CURE OF EVERY FORM OF DISEASE book.

'Open it,' say Gommel.

Howul try the teeny grey key in the lock. He pretend it wont turn.

'It stick again,' he say. 'It need more oil.'

'More pigsarse,' say Gommel.

They leave the house and walk slow and quiet through the village. Howul know every dip, every bump, every point and every puddle the ground have. Gommel hold on to him so he do not trip. Hims breath is weak and fast.

'Where you take me?' whisper Howul.

'Nobody Beach,' say Gommel.

'Why?'

'So you can scape, isnit?'

Gommel gasp for breath as he say it. Perhap he like Howul. Perhap he want to help him. When he have learn Howul to read, he have hiss cough laugh plenty.

To go more fast, Howul offer to pick him up and carry him. And the stick and red box. Gommel agree.

Howul have watch boats arrive at Blanow. Alway they is fill with dead or near dead but if thems boats can arrive then other boats can leave. Perhap Gommel have one for him at Nobody Beach.

Since many day, no one can reach it. But now the sea is out far enough for them to get round to it. It is all sea slime and grey slate but, because Howul have spend such good time here with Jen, for a moment hims grump mind ease.

Howul set Gommel on hims feet again and give him back box and stick. Kiss and love is not why he is bring here. Gommel lead him slow and careful to where cypress trees cover the cliff at the back. He push the stick against some branches. Again they move away to reveal a wood door. He open it. Another cave.

On a shelf of the door is some spark sticks and candles. Gommel get Howul to light one. Shadows make thems faces sharp as the cave rock.

'There is a boat for me?' Howul ask.

'For sure,' say Gommel. 'But first is more best. You know I alway do what I can for you, Howul? Try to make life more good for you?'

'Yes.'

'So I have make it here also. Your daughter.'

'Erin?'

'You have other daughter?'

Hiss. Cough.

'She is here. She can scape with you. She wait for you here.'

No cyclone can ever hit Howul as hard as these words. No honey is as sweet.

'Where?' he say.

Gommel point into cave with stick.

'They put her there for not want to be White Dress Woman.'

'What you mean? What they do to her?'

'She is Okay. Now you can scape together.'

'In boat?'

'Yes. I take you there.'

Howul look into the cave entrance. Part of him want to rush in and save hims daughter. Part of him is scare to. What have they do to her?

He call out her name.

'Shhh,' say Gommel. 'We must be quiet. They will kill me if they know I do this for you.'

'They hurt her?'

'No. But they tie her up. She is Okay, I promise. You can free her. She tell me how much she love you.'

'Erin say this?'

'Yes. And what good father you is to her. She need you now, Howul.'

Howul is please she say these things. All he get from her is Ash and Shite look, tell to stop bother and pester, tell to let her be.

'She say this to you?'

'For sure. But to save her we must be quick.'

Of a sudden a cold hand squeeze hims heart. Only person Erin ever tell about what she feel is her mother. So why have she say this to Gommel?

Howul is hims fathers son. He know billy bully when he hear it.

He wait a moment as new thinkings crowd hims brain. Then he decide.

'Give me your stick,' he say.

'Why?'

'The cave floor is wet with sea slime. It will stop me fall over.'

'I need it. Others walk there without fall over. Go in and get your daughter.'

Without the stick Gommel cannot close the door. He cannot shut Howul in. So Howul ask for it again and still he do not pass it over. Howul take it from him. Next he walk slow into the cave. It is long, narrow and damp. The sea slime floor slope down and fill with water. He is wet up to hims knees when he reach the most far part of it. The light of candle show what is ahead. Only rock. He call out her name. Unless she is now deaf or is also turn to rock, she do not wait for him here. Then he see her. Stick thin shoulders press against the cave wall. Stick thin legs skew out in front of her. Head loll forward. Face cover by hair. He go to her.

'Baby,' he say and touch her hand.

It is cold. He rub her skin to warm it. Round her neck is the ribbon she wear alway. Colour of rowan berrys, two fingers wide, Jens ribbon. Under it is red marks. Someone have strangle her with it. He hold her and kiss her cold face. Erin.

A moan scape from him that grow into a scream.

He blink fast, take short breaths, decide what to do. Carry her out of the cave, warm her up, make her well again. He lift her in hims arms.

Gommel have drag himself half way across the Beach by the time he reach the cave door. He lay Erin down, hold her hands and blow on them to warm her. He smile at her, talk to her, encourage her.

Gommel shout for help but is too out of breath and weak of voice to top the sound of the waves.

"He get help for you,' say Howul. 'Help is here soon.'

He do not want to hurt her by say what is true. It is not Erin Gommel want to save. It is himself.

Howul kiss her again, hug her and let her go. Soon he catch up with Gommel. He grab him by hims white smoke hair and pull back hims head.

'You do not have to kill her.'

'I do not kill her. I will talk to Mister Yorath so you can stay in Blanow. All is good.'

Before he promise boat and scape for him and Erin. Now it is talk to Mister Yorath. Evil old fuck. Howul still have hims stick. To stop him from get help, he raise it and crash it down on hims head. Blood make dark hims hair. He try to say something. Howul hit him again. Soon he is quiet. Howul have never hit anyone before. He feel no shame to hurt a cripple old man. He get what is deserve.

The sea is still far enough out for Howul to walk back to Blanow. For why? So he is on trial again? So Tall Nole can kill him?

He go back to Erin and make sure she rest well. Arms cross, eyes close, ribbon tie in her hair again. He kiss her one last time.

Light have begin to creep over the top of the cliffs. It tell all of Blanow to wake up, find him, catch him. But where to go?

Sea is fill with sea monisters. All of Blanow avoid it. Even Si and Robut stand on shore as they fish. Anyone who go in sea is eat or drown.

Every part of him is weary and hurt. He want to close hims eyes, stop, lie down, give up. Above him the night stars dim and fade. Hims father say that, if you look at them careful, alway you know where you is. He know just where he is. Sick in hims heart, alone, desperate. In deepshite.

#

JOURNEY

The oildrums of Pomegranate Face and the others is still on mud shore where they is drag by Tall Nole and Droo. No one have use them for anything yet. They is not the boat Gommel have promise and it is dangerous for him to go get them. He do not want to. But what else can he do?

Big Tris is on The Green but is too busy with pattycakes to notice him. No one else is here yet. One oildrum still have some rope round it. He tie it onto hims back and return with it to Nobody Beach. He go where sea is, loose rope so now he face front and throw himself in. Water wash round oildrum but he keep above. He do same as People Before do who try to reach Blanow. He splash with hands to move himself forward. Even without splash, the oildrum still move. It is like the sea want to help him. Monisters to feed, perhap.

Before long he is far enough away so no one from Blanow can see him. Snake, rat, stiffneck disease etcetera etcetera. Challenge. Trial. And now sea. For true, he is the most lucky of most unlucky men. To show how lucky he is, heavy rain now smash down on him. He turn over and catch some in hims mouth. The more bad things is, the more hard he fight. He will scape or kill all monisters. No wave will drown him. And who ever do this to hims daughter will pay.

#

He drift in the water one day then two. As he pass land he look for somewhere to splash to and climb out. But all is steep grey cliffs that cut through water like huge knife blades.

At night he freeze. Lucky Howul.

Those who reach Blanow by boat is alway near death. Alway they have travel many day. And alway they reach Blanow past Place for Lookout, not past Nobody Beach. Water push them into Blanow. For him it is different. From Nobody Beach, water push him away.

He remember of course what Blanow do to People Outside. Will others welcome him with food, water, a woman? Like fuckery. Still he prefer them or sea to kill him than Tall Nole.

By day three, he have find way to sit with feet in water.

Pain for hims back and arse is now less. Rain may smash down or sun burn or wind make waves more big or sea monister attack, but at least hims back and arse is less bad.

He remember how he have shove pouch in hims britches before he leave hims house. He have before hide many things in slats – herbs, pattycake, small pieces of potato and scrag meat. Is pouch safe? Hims keepsakes, teeny books and pencils? Hims clothes is all heavy with water but the pouch protect when it rain before. He go to check. Then, of a sudden, the sea round him begin to shake. He lean forward to see what is there. A grey shadow move slow up toward him. A sea monister. Hims huge mouth spread wide apart ready to bite or swallow. Hims cold black eyes stare at Howul who lift hims feet out of water. Then, as he get more near, he drop hims nose and sink down again. Every part of Howul tremble. Part fear, part cold. Soon the monister return. This time, think Howul, this time. But again the creature appoach and leave. And again. Then the sea calm. To this monister perhap Howul is a gurnard fish – for every piece to chew there is fourteen bones to spit out.

Soon perhap another appear who like gurnard fish more. The cliffs is far away but he splash hard to get more close.

Rage boil inside him. Everything he have, everything he do, some shooky arsehole try to take it from him. A cyclone. A shitebag Brenin. A evil old man. A monister.

The rage make him splash more fierce till after much time he reach cliffs. Water push him against them so flesh is scrape from hims shoulder. He shout and tell all to gofuck. If he must die, he die angry, not fright nor defeat.

Howul know that nothing go right, not even easy thing, till after you try and try and think all is brack. Without you shout and scream, answer alway is hide from you. So only now, after he scream at cliffs and is scrape by them, he find what he need. A thin gap like crack in glass you only see when is hold to light. Thin but big enough for oildrum. Where fast water flow through.

The water take him beyond cliffs to a clean still pond. He crawl onto tall grass beside. He try to stand up but hims arms and legs is too bloat. Hims red raw skin is burn to buggery. The grass hide him and sleep soon have him.

#

As he wake up, he throw off mildew blankets and listen for rat. Only there is no blankets nor rat. Tall grass instead. He can hear redback lizards and grasshops and a stream that bring fresh water into the pond. These is all real. He smell rosemary and elderberry. Because he have never leave Blanow before, he expect outside all to be new and different. But grass is still grass. Water is still water. There is only one sun. Gold season in Blanow is gold season here. When he move away from tall grass he find strawberrys, spinach, mint, lettuce, beans. It is a place of plenty. Same but more. He fill hims stomach and drink water from stream. Bricks on ground show where one time is house. People Before have live here.

The snake skin is still round hims hair. The white bangle is still round hims wrist but all hims clothes is daggy and shonked. Hims shoes have wash away, hims shirt is tatters, hims britches is rags. All is more chafe than wear. He remember pouch again and hate himself for not remember more soon. He have shame hims father, mother, woman, daughter by forget.

Hims hands shake as he check the wood slats where he have place it between. Still safe. He take it out. Outside is soak but all inside is still dry. He look careful at keepsakes, kiss them and put them back. The stone Erin have give him go in last.

Next he kiss the teeny books that have save hims life. Mister Yorath want so bad to know what is in them, what Howul can learn him about others in Blanow. Why? In Big House he have see how Brenin live. Cut off, hide away, everything give and say to him by others he do not trust. More he know, more safe he must feel. Or else he just like to get most recent goss.

Howul have all he need here. Food, water, tall grass for sleep. Hims arms and legs is soon normal size again. He follow the stream inland from the pond. This take him to a steep hill that rise up with bare earth, white rocks, low trees, scrubby plants and shy flowers. Nettles here is still nettles. Daisys is still daisys. Comfrey is still comfrey.

He go to top of hill and look round. No fires, no houses, no People Outside.

He return to pond. As it grow dark he put together twigs and branches and dry leafs and scrape two firestones till they spark. Soon he have a good fire. Because hims clothes is so shooky, he take them off and throw them on fire. He wind snake skin in hims hair tight round pouch to keep it in place. He lie naked near fire under more dry leafs and sleep the sleep of the safe.

#

Next morning he take out book and fill some pages with what have hap and all he have lose. Challenge. Tinfoods. Red hair woman. Tall Nole. Nobody Beach. Sea. As he write he feel nothing. It is as if it all hap to someone else. He do not yet want to believe it all hap to him.

When Jen die, he can think of nothing else for many, many day. He see her everywhere. He hold her. He talk to her. She smile at him and warm him. Any bad is bury with her. She is never piss with him, never nudge him to stop from snore, never make bad smell. Still now her love can warm him. With Erin, there is only bad. How he have not save her. How much pain he give her. How twig thin her arms is. The White Dress. Her in the cave, head loll forward, face cover by hair. Hims son Idris who die before her and is not let live because of her. Only bad.

With Challenges, Nobody Beach, sea, sea monisters, snake bite, diseases etcetera etcetera, he have now scape death more time than he can remember. Others get damp or cut thems finger and straight after they is in Field of Black. Not him. He piss on death then life make him suffer again. Any good that hap to him, alway it is take away soon after. Any good he do go bad. For why? He have no idea. All he know for sure is that nothing Death can throw at him can kill him. He have become like man in story call Sissypuss. He push heavy rock up hill and, as he near the top, it roll back down and crush him. But do not kill him. Next day, he push again and same thing hap. And next day and next day and next.

He need Jen to help stop him from think all this.

Instead of cross legs, breathe slow and mind walk with bumblybees and flutterbys, he find new way. He write down the story hims father Garith tell call FORSE. When others tell it, some make the bad things less bad and more easy for good people to stop. Some make bad things only hap to bad people and only good to good. Some botch how they tell it and what they add so no one givashite what hap. No one tell it as good as Howuls father. He make it so, even though bad things hap, still you have hope that, if they hap to you, you can defeat them. He do not make the bad people brute. They is like people you know and like person you can be. Choice give hope.

Howul cannot do this when he tell FORSE. With him, bad people win, good people is crush. Or they win a little and is then crush big. The best person is alway like how he want to be but more young. Someone who, by try to do good, make all more bad. He have never write it before, only tell it. This is how it start when he write it now. This is how he spell it also. Way we spell things is more how People Before spell. Perhap Howul forget how some words is spell or perhap he think hims spell is more good.

FORSE

People Before is soft hands people. Cleen face people. Round arse people. Brain people.

People Before think, eet, tork, sleep. When they do sumthin, make sumthin, all is as much use as spit in sea. Shirt that do not keep yoo dry. Lump of mettul yoo can not kill anythin with. Peece of wood that is fantsy carve, do not burn.

People Before is many people, live in many places. One is village call Ulderun. Here is alway cleen water. Potatos, hunny is plenty. Trees throw froot into yor hands as yoo walk under them. Ulderun people is Gold People.

Brenin of Ulderun is woman. Thick brown hair stand up on hed like crab shell. Clothes is wite, smell of roses. Fingernails is barnacle hard, long. Name is Prinsess.

For fifteen yeer, only water she drink is cool, cleen. Food is eggs cook with spinitch and tomatos, pidjin roast on fire with peppers and mushrumps, fresh mackril bake with corianda, lemon, chesnuts, other meet, other fish, other froot, other vegitibil cook any way she want.

Till one day People Outside arrive in Ulderun. People Before is soft hands brain people. People Outside is cold hart big fist people.

Gold People have not meet People Outside before. They point to apples, peetchs, strorberrys, cherrys, cleen water.

'All for yoo also,' say Prinsess.

Brenin of People Outside have mettul over head. It hide all ecsept lips and chin. Over hands is black mettul gloves, over feet is black mettul boots, over chest, arms, legs is also black mettul. Name is Deep. He speak cwiert. Every one listen.

'If yoo want to live, yoo will do only what I tell yoo,' Deep say.

Gold People smile at him, nod. He bend down to snotnose call Arnul. Arnul smile as Deep put fingers of mettul gloves round neck and scweeze. Arnul smile till he stop to breethe. He die and think all is game.

Gold People run forwid to help. People Outside slash with knifes till they step back.

Deep take out small black mettul scware. He look thru window on it then speek cwiert to other People Outside. Soon Gold People is carry this, get that, dig this, fill that, pull, push, swet, heeve, work like they never work before. Most what they do is bild sumthin with corrygate iron, steel, wood, plasty. Deth weppun. Plans for it Deep see when he look thru window of black mettul scware.

In Ulderun also is young man call Sky. Eyes is more wide open than every one elses, like every thing sprise him. Some time yoo see first grow of a tree, know it will alway stay true. So is with Sky. Every thing he say, think, even when for first time, every one can see is good.

After People Outside arrive, every thing Sky do is rong. They give him wood to carry. He drop it. They give him hammer to brack rocks with. He brack own finger. They give him water or piss to drink. He drink piss.

Insted of make angry, wat he do rong make them laff. Other Gold People they kick, beet, kill for no reesun. If Sky follow them, they let him. It please them to see him drop more wood, drink more piss. He is fayvrit idjurt. Ecsept when Deep is neer. Then they kick, beet Sky to show how cold hart big fist they is.

Every nite Deep give black mettul scware to Fin _ a man so strong every muscule have muscule. Every nite Sky follow Fin, watch as he walk over to big wite box, put mettul scware inside, close it. On Fins arm is many numbers tattoo. Press numbers into wite box, it lock. It take longtime because so many numbers. Then Fin go to hall where People Outside eet, sleep.

Trees throw off thems leefs, brown seesun become wite seesun. Wind blow so cold birds fall ded to erth. Fast water is deep ice. One nite Sky watch as Fin stand by wite box, stamp feet, clap hands to keep warm. He put black mettul scware in box, close it.

Tattoo is cover by warm sleeve, hands is in thick gloves. He start to take off glove, stop. How cold go hims fingers if he press numbers. He look round, make sure alone, do not see Sky. Walk away.

Sky have fingers of ice. Blow on them, more ice grow. He push them under arms till feel tips again, open box, take out scware.

Nex day, People Outside sertch all Ulderun for it. Gold People stand in lines, is ask where it is. If persun do not say, Deep *slash throte with flint knife. One persun then nex then nex till Prinsess stand before. He show blood drentch blade.*

'Kill all of us,' she say. 'We have what yoo want. Yoo will never see it again.'

Rain begin to spit down on him. Soon yellow stripes light up above him and thunder crash onto the ground round him. Hims fire is wash away. He stand up, scoop up clodges of mud, throw them at where the stripes flash. Shout. Scream. Fight. Defy. Deny.

#

When he wake up, a rat same size as hims right foot is bite on it. He stand up and kick hard to fling it off but it wont let go of hims big toesy. He find a rock and crush its back. Rat is perfect for scrag soup. Howul go to put it in hims rocksack for Big Tris. He stop. There is no Big Tris. There is no rocksack.

He examine the bite. Part of the toesy is eat away. He wash it in the stream then press comfrey leafs hard against it. He lift it up and rest it on a stone. If he stay here another night and rain again wash out the fire, for sure there will be more rats. If he walk far, the wound will split again.

He pack hims foot with more comfrey leafs bind together with long grass. He do the same with hims left foot so it is protect from stones and thorns. After he have eat, he begin to walk. By the time he reach the top of the hill, the comfrey leafs is soak with blood. The ground drop away a little with more bare earth and white rocks. He go in straight line for longtime till the earth rise steep again to top of another hill. Beyond again is no sign of People Outside. But animals is here he have never see before. The size of snotnoses, they have gull thin legs and hair down to thems knees. Thems faces is narrow, thems ears big and flat. Behind thems ears, sharp spikes point back. As he limp toward them, they retreat from him then stare back through wet, pink eyes. He cannot decide if they is stupid or evil. He have never see so much meat on any creature before. He throw a rock at one which easy skip out of the way. To kill them, Howul need a sharp spear and luck. He do not expect neither soon.

He sit, chew camomile leafs and keep hims foot up on a rock. When he is rest, he limp on up next hill. On top is metal trees each as tall as ten Big House. Near the ground, they is like silverbirchs that have lose all thems branches. More high up, three giant metal sycamore seeds stick out from them and whirl and spin. As they spin, they hum. Thems trunks is wet cold metal. When he touch them, hims hand shake. People Before have make them. He do not know what for.

Where the ground slope down again is rows of pine trees set close together in straight lines. They fill every hollow, every dip, every ridge, every flat, every rise. They make thick the air with thems rich heavy scent. Any way he walk ahead, he walk through them. He find a branch he can use as stick then keep walk straight ahead. He see another animal he have not see before. The size of a pigeon, he have giant eyes, a grey back, a white stomach and a grey feather tail that he throw and flick behind.

Howul tread soft toward him with stone ready to throw but the animal hear before he get near. He do not scurry away like a rat. He do not fly away like a pigeon. He speed away like hims tail is on fire, throw hims body against a tree and slide round so Howul cannot see him. Perhap hims stomach is stickystuff.

He limp on till at last the lines of pine trees is brack up and a wood of cypress, maple, beech, holly and oak is before him. He sit down beneath a maple where the earth is damp and soft. Apart from the leafs round hims feet and the snake skin, he is still naked. He do not think this worry the trees and creatures he pass.

He remove the leafs from hims right foot, wipe it clean with rain water and pack it again with comfrey. He do not look too close in case he see anything too bad. He stand up again and limp on. Then he smell wood smoke. People Outside. Avoid them? Not him. Not now. He is Howul. Every death he face he piss on.

He follow the smoke to a clearing. In it is two men, a woman and a neat wood fire.

The men wear dark green robes that gleam like fish scales and cover from thems shoulders to thems knees. Both have same wide shoulders, push up noses and big foreheads.

Father and son, think Howul. They use axes to chop pine
branches into more and more small pieces. As they do this,
no part of them look ache nor shonked. Thems hair shine,
thems teeth gleam, thems faces have a light that is not just
fire glow. More late on, he find out they is call Emlin and
Steve. For now, they is just two men he hate same way he
hate Jack and Julie.

The woman, Beth, poke at the fire with a stick. She wear a
thin shiny black robe that stay close to her skin. She have
long black hair soft as gull down and eyes that is acorn
brown. Her skin shine like wet pebbles and her teeth is
straight as ice. Perfect round titties with no sag nor droop. As
Howul look at her he have one hundred year and is more ugly
than rotted seaweed. He hate her also.

On the ground close to the fire is some fresh cook onions.
The smell pull him to them. The People Outside who reach
Blanow is already weak from starve and burn. But all People
Outside is menace so Blanow kill them. Will they do same to
him? Offer water, offer onions then smash hims skull with
rock?

Of usual, he should avoid them, move on.

The smell of cook onion fill hims nose again. All sense is
push out. He is Howul Sissypuss who nothing can kill. He
drop branch on ground, hurry forward, pick up a onion and
hurry away with it as best as hims botch foot allow. Onion is
fierce hot so he pass it from hand to hand.

'Stop,' shout one of the men from behind him.

He hobble on as fast as he can and hear thems footsteps as
they chase him. The onion burn hims fingers and he drop it.
He do not want to lose it. He try to pick it up and see son
Steve run toward him with a axe in hims right hand. He stand
up and face him with fists raise.

'Is there any more of you?' say Steve.

Hims voice is quiet and easy. What he ask is what Mister
Yorath ask before they kill People Outside.

'Yes,' say Howul. 'Thirty.'

He swing hims fist at Steves head. And miss. Beth and
Emlin join them.

'You want food?' say Emlin.

Howul watch the axe in Steves hand, ready to grab for it or
jump away.

'Madbad,' say Beth.

She say it like it is hims name. He correct her.

'Howul, son of Garith, son of Piter, son of Nominus.'

'We will not hurt you, Howul,' say Emlin.

'Why not?'

They smile at him like he is dear silly snotnose.

'You want food. We have enough to share,' say Beth.

Howuls stomach make noise like water boil inside it. Beth point back toward fire.

'Eat with us,' she say.

She hold out her clean, soft, perfect hand. Naked rotted seaweed, Howul take it.

No axe fall on him as he eat all the onions. Steve kick dirt onto the fire to put it out. He, Emlin and Beth place the wood they have cut in huge clothbags and drag them along the ground. A path lead out of the clearing and over a mound of lush grass. Howul move forward then stop as the path sink and rise in front of him.

'You is Okay?' say Beth.

She catch him as he fall. Her soft skin smell of jasmine and camomile. Hims eyes fill with black.

#

TANGRISH

Heat is in every part of him. Dark shapes attack him, disappear when he hit out at them, attack again. Shakes rattle hims body. He sweat rivers.

Jen put her hand on hims forehead then over hims eyes to close them.

He feel warm, light, calm, safe.

'Howie,' she say.

As he reach out for her he open hims eyes. She is not there. The dark shapes return.

#

Everything is clean and sharp and clear. He do not shake. The thick blanket over him smell of lemon and pine. He sit up slow. Nothing hurt. Death again he have piss on. He look to see where he is. Above, under, everywhere round him is wood that shine and gleam. Shelfs, drawers, a table, benches, a stool with plumpy cushions to sit on, the bed he lie on. All is pack in neat together like a small Big House. Through the unbrack glass windows he can see daylight and grass.

Beth is here also. She sit on a bench and do not realise he have wake up. She have yellow, red and blue beads in her hair, a white shirt with no smudge nor dirt in it and a red skirt that is without rip nor tear. Her face is without fret. Like people in Ulderun before People Outside arrive, she is Gold People. Everything easy.

She sense he look at her.

'You is Okay?'

'Yes.'

'You have bad fever. We treat you.'

She stand up, lean over him and put her hand on hims forehead.

'Good,' she say.

She take her hand away and smile. He remember hims foot. He look down at where the blanket cover it.

'Foot is Okay also,' she say.

She hold up a dark green robe that gleam and shine like the ones Emlin and Steve have wear.

'If you want to, when you is ready, you can wear this.'

She lay it down, throw him one more big smile and leave.

Unlike Jack and Julie, she share with him good things she have. He hate her less now. But he wonder what she want back.

He push away the blanket and stand up. Hims toe have not grow back but is heal over well. Rest of him is all sharp bone. He put on the warm, soft robe. It have a pocket. He have never wear anything so warm nor soft nor have a pocket.

He reach for the snake skin in hims hair. It is not there. He move quick to rage and is ready to smash all in front of him before he see it on shelf near hims warm, soft bed. Next to it is the leather pouch. He open it. Keepsakes, teeny books and pencils is all safe inside. He put the pouch in the pocket and tie the snake skin back on.

On the table is a plate with spinach, potatos and meat that is not rat nor pigeon. It taste of smoke and chew as easy as long cook celery. Hims stomach want more but he stop before it return anything. Hims head is dizzy so he sit on the bench where Beth have sit. He smell her jasmine and camomile.

When hims head is clear again, he push open the door of this small Big House. Wood steps drop to the ground. Hims brain tell hims legs to move. They do not hear. Then it tell them to stay still. Too late. He slide down the steps and land on hims arse.

Gold People rush over to help. Thems clothes is many different colours and all look new make. The sun blast down as they cluck and coo over him like Glend with baby Murf. They help him stand.

Name of this place, they tell him, is Tangrish. All Howul know of People Outside is they must be kill before they kill you. But these is more good to him than Blanow people. In Blanow hims life is cadge and hide and cheat and hustle and starve. Here they is care and kind, feed and make warm. Why?

The Gold People lead him to a building with a roof so high it hurt hims neck to see top of it. Inside all is cool. Like in Big House, spiders webs with pieces of glass on them hang from the ceiling and throw light on everyone. People sit on benches with tall wood backs. Beth lead him to a empty bench near the front. Before they get there he see three boy teens. They is different ages. When they look at him, they all drop thems chins and open thems mouths same way. They have same shape lips and noses also.

Not possible, think Howul. But the thinking stay.

'Brothers?' he ask Beth.

'Yes,' she say.

As Howul walk on, the most old brother say this to the others –

'Madbad.'

Howuls first brother arrive when he have five year. He remember the big stomach of hims mother Mags and the noises she make when he is born. For one season, she never leave him. She hold him, talk to him, give him milk. Howul is ignore. Then hims father Garith tell him they have take hims brother to Field of Black.

'He sleep now,' say Garith.

Howul worry he will wake up and come back. He do not want him to come back and take hims mother from him again.

'When he come back?' Howul ask hims father.

'Never,' say Garith. 'The earth is gentle blanket for him.'

Howul is please.

Hims next brother is when he have eight year. After two season Jims and Droo come for him. This time Howul do not want him to go. He like the smell of him and snuffly way he breathe and how hims big eyes watch everything Howul do. He make hims mother laugh and this please him to see.

'I will hide him,' Howul say to hims father. 'They will not find him.'

'No,' say Garith. 'The earth will soon be a gentle blanket for him.'

He get the baby from Mags and take him to Jims and Droo.

If they is in Tangrish, he and both hims brothers may all live.

Howul sit down on the bench which Beth have lead him to and look round. There is plenty of other brothers and sisters here. Father, mother, brothers, sisters share the same bench. Some benches have eight people.

He have think Gold People must want something from him. Why else do they not kill him? But when some here have so many brothers and sisters, perhaps one more person is no matter to them. In Blanow, everyone need and only a few get. Here it seem everyone get and no one need. When to live is more easy, to give is more easy also.

Howuls bench is just for him. The bench in front of him also have just one person. He sit, chew seeds and spit out the husks. The floor round him is wet with them.

Howul look close at him. Small blue eyes and a nose big enough for snotnoses to hide under. Rid, son of Owen, son of Gordy. Only man in Blanow with a face more cod fish ugly and nose more big than hims own. For the last two year Howul have think he is dead. Everyone say that when Mister Yorath die Rid will be new Brenin. Then he disappear. Howul and Rid never like each other. Howul think Rid is a craxy shitebag. Rid think Howul is a arsepain grumpscrut. Both is right.

'How you get here, Rid?' say Howul.

Rid spit out some more husks.

'Mind your bizzy and gofuck,' he say.

Same old Rid.

Of a sudden everyone stand up. A woman walk in with feathers in her hair and white stripes on her face. Her body is big with muscules. Clothes in many different pieces fit close over her. She walk quick and in no time is right before Howul. She take hims face in both hands. She push her fingers into hims cheeks and through hims long clodgy hair as if by this she can know hims every thinking.

'You is from Blanow?' she ask and let go.

Howul nod.

'Blanow?' she ask again.

Howul nod again. She laugh.

'Blanow?'

Howul think he is talk to by a nutjob.

'Yes, Blanow,' he say.

'What is you call?'

'Howul.'

'I is Featherwoman. All here welcome you with open heart.'

She lean forward and hug him. He let her but do not want it. When she release him he glare at her. She lean forward and hug him again. Now he realise. Her eyes move but do not see. She turn away and face everyone else.

'Let us give thanks,' she say.

She close her eyes and everyone else except Howul and Rid do the same. All is quiet and still.

'Let us give thanks for who we is and what we have,' say Featherwoman. 'For the food we eat and the water we drink, for the clothes we wear, for the sun that shine on us and the sun we shine on each other. Let us give thanks that we still live and for the safe recovery of Howul. Let us give thanks.'

She stamp her right foot then her left foot on the ground. Everyone else do the same. She do it again and soon everyone else is stamp, stamp, stamp like floor is cover with ants. Then she stop and hold up her arms. They stop and do the same. They stay like this longtime, silent, arms up.

All nutjobs.

#

No one here go without vegetables nor fruit nor pattycakes nor eggs nor meat. No one steal wood. The metal trees Howul have see make electrics like Mister Yoraths fridge use. It mean that, even at night, all in Tangrish is warm and light.

Before, apart from when he heal sick or is with Jen or Erin, Howul most time avoid people. Now all day he is with father Emlin, son Steve and hims woman Beth. Every morning they go over the mound of lush grass, along path and into the same clearing where first he see them. Every morning when they get there Emlin say –

'No rest for the wicked.'

They chop branches from pine trees and cut them into wood pieces. Then they scrape off bark, leafs and twigs.

If it rain, they smile. If wood they cut is botch, they smile. If bramble scratch them, they smile. From time to time they ask Howul –

'Is you Okay?'

When he complain of rain or botch or bramble scratchs, Emlin say –

'Good is not good without bad.'

Or Steve say –

'Let us give thanks that most time we is dry.'

Or Beth say –

'When bramble scratch me, Steve kiss it good for me. One day, Howul, someone kiss it good for you.'

And all smile. Thems easy cheer make Howul want to throw rocks at them. Now when they ask –

'Is you Okay?'

– he chop another branch and pretend he do not hear.

At sun high they stop, eat potatos and onions and drink water. Then Emlin say –

'No time like the present,'

and they go back to work. Then, as the sky begin to grey Emlin say –

'Now let us call it a day,'

and they put the wood in the huge clothbags and carry them back so people can make axe handles, knife handles, bows, arrows, sticks, wood plates etcetera etcetera. When they get back, Gold People stop what they do and ask 'All is Okay?' and they say 'Yes' then ask people 'Is all Okay with you also?' and they say 'Yes'.

Every 'Yes' and 'Okay' is like no one have ever say it before. All is talky and smily and chuffy except for Howul who still pretend not to hear and want to throw more rocks.

They let him stay in small Big House. Tangrish have many of them, all new make with pine wood. In the evening they drink cool, clean water and eat.

Beth might say 'Today is good weather, isnit?' and Shiel might say 'Yes. And I have see two woodypecks'. Emlin might say 'Is Martin able to mend hims spade?' and Owin might say 'Yes and now it as good as before'. Then everyone go into the high roof building which is call The Shapple and do footstamps.

No one tell storys here. They never ask Howul of Blanow and hims life there. Thems life in Tangrish is already so fill with weather and woodypecks and well mend spades they dont need anything else. Or else the footstamps have shake off bits of thems brains.

At start, Howul is glad to chop wood, eat and drink, sleep. Hims mind is fill only with will wood cut good, clean good, dry good. He sleep well. But the more day he is in Tangrish, the more bad thinkings return. Hims dreams fill with what he never want to see again. Thin shoulders. Stick thin legs. Head loll forward. Cold hand.

When he think of Erin he feel angry and weak. Bad father. Bad life. Bad death. Evil slimefucks kill her and he have let them.

Only way he can shake off hims own hurt is when he think how much he will hurt them back. But when? How? With what? He need to find a way.

#

Gold People do not get sick nor even pretend to get sick. But Madbad Rid is alway sick. He lie down a lot and smoke ganja a lot but some how this never cure him. Because he is alway sick, Gold People give him easy work. Instead of cut wood or fetch water or make fire, all he do is sort seeds that others collect for him from different plants and flowers.

First time they meet in Tangrish, Rid tell Howul to mind hims bizzy and gofuck. Every time they meet after, Howul ask –

'Is you Okay?'

– and Rid say same as before. It please Howul to annoy him this way.

This evening, as footstamps end, Howul ask Rid –

'Is you Okay?'

This time, what Rid say is different.

'The tea you make in Blanow,' he say. 'You can make it here?'

'I make many teas,' say Howul.

'What you make when everyone get sick, isnit?'

He make camomile tea one time when everyone have bad stomach after Big Tris do not proper wash samphire.

'You is sick? Perhaps you work too hard.'

'You have tea?'

Rid have alway hate him. But if he help Rid, perhaps he will hate him less. And Rid is only person in Tangrish who also know what Challenge and Field of Black is and what it is to be Madbad.

'I will make tea you need, same as I make in Blanow. I will help you,' he say.

Howul take him to a room in The Shapple behind where the footstamps hap. It is for sick people so no one use it. In it is two beds with thin cloths stretch tight over them, blankets on top and metal legs under. Howul ask Rid to sit on bed.

'I do not want bed. I want tea.'

'Not all teas is good for all things. If I give you wrong tea, I make you more bad.'

He check Rids eyes, tongue and hair. He ask him what he eat and how much ganja he smoke.

'Not much,' he say. 'I eat what others eat.'

Howul nod and smile even though he know Rid talk gobbledybollocks. Ganja some time make a stomach bad. Howul can tell Rids bad is more than that but do not know why. He bring him valerian tea.

'You must stay here where I can watch you,' he say. 'It is good we is now friends.'

Rid sit then lie on one bed. The tea calm him and soon he sleep. To show how much he care, Howul sleep in next bed.

In Blanow Rid is suppose to become Brenin. He is high up and know much Howul do not. If Howul can find it out, this may help him get back and kill those who kill Erin. By help and heal him, he hope Rid will trust him more and tell him more. But first he must understand what really make him sick. To do this, he must watch him without hims know.

Next morning, he send Rid back home then go find Emlin.

'I cannot go to the clearing today,' he say. 'Rid is not Okay.'

'Okay,' say Emlin.

Rids small Big House is away from everyone elses in a dell of hawthorn, holly, bramble and laurel. Howul hide himself in laurel but not before other plants have scratch him to buggery. He bleed, wait and watch.

Rid sit outside the house at a pine table. On it is seeds for him to sort in piles then put in little clothbags. Hims feet is on the table and he lean back. In one hand is a ganja stick. In the other is something he put in hims mouth and chew.

Of a sudden Howul hear voices and footsteps close to him.

Rid hear them also, lean forward, drop ganja stick and start to sort seeds.

A voice call out Rids name. It is Featherwoman. She arrive with four men. She hold arm of one so she do not trip on anything but move so fast you think he hold on to her.

'Ready?' say Featherwoman.

Rid know she cannot see him but still move fast like he

want to please her. He go over to some tall grass close to the house and lift up a thick flat piece of wood that is hide in it. It cover a hole which he now go down. After wait, the men pull rope up from the hole. Attach to it is empty blue plastycrate. When they have lift up four crates, Rid climb back up. He and Featherwoman say something Howul cannot hear. Featherwoman and the others leave and take crates with them. Rid climb back down into the hole again.

No one have see Howul.

Howul wait a moment then go over to the table where Rid pretend to work. He examine what Rid eat. Pieces of dry fly agaric mushroom. They look like bad skin burn. Put them in oil and rub them on your face, they keep moskits away. Chew them and your mind travel to strange new places. Chew too many and your stomach fill with cramps.

He hear a noise from where Rid disappear and hurry back to where he hide before. Rid go into hims house and return with tinfoods. He use a knife to open them and tip grey slushimush from them straight into hims mouth. Then he eat more fly agarics and light hims ganja stick. Howul now know what have make Rid sick. But he want to know what is down hole also. To do this he must return when Rid is not here. For usual, a go-to person for medicine try to make someone well. Not Howul, not now. He plan to keep Rid sick.

As night reach Tangrish, Rid come to The Shapple. He do not footstamp but go straight to the room for sick people. When Howul find him, sweat drip from hims forehead and hims face is white as new teeth.

'Is you Okay?' Howul ask.

Rid groan.

'What you eat today?'

'What you think I eat? Same as everyone, isnit?'

Howul make him lie down on the bed then put hims ear gentle against hims stomach.

'You eat same as everyone?'

'Yes.'

'Spinach? Pattycakes? Meat?'

'Yes.'

Howul rest hims hand on the middle of Rids stomach.

'Today you have eat tinfood and mushrooms. And smoke ganja,' he say.

Rid look at him amaze. Howul give hims stomach gentle push. Rid scream out with pain.

'Do that hurt?'

'What you think?'

Rid groan. Howul press hims hand on hims stomach again. Rid scream. Howul know that the more Rid suffer, the more like he is to do what is ask.

'The mushrooms have poison you.'

'I have eat them before. They do no harm.'

'It depend how many you eat. And what kind. How many you eat today?'

'Not many.'

'And you smoke ganja?'

'Not much.'

'You drink any water?'

'Water cannot poison me.'

'Water is good. You drink any?'

'Of course I drink water, isnit.'

Howul look away like there is something bad he do not want to tell Rid. Rid sit up and grab hims wrists.

'What?' he say.

'As your friend, Rid, I want to help you. But this is not good. If you do not do just what I tell you, the poison will kill you. And soon.'

'You serious?'

'How you feel?'

'Soon? How long?'

'Already there is enough inside you to kill you. This is why you must lie still for many hour to keep poison where it is. If you go anywhere, you move it around and make it spread. Wait here, lie still and do not move. I bring you something that help stop you from die. But I cannot hide it from you, my friend. You is bad sick.'

Howul go make some tea and bring it back to him. A tea to keep him wake not help him sleep.

'Drink this.'

'You say I must lie still.'

'There is special places on your back I can tap as you drink which stop poison from move. But only for short while. Other time you must lie still.'

He tap Rids back in many places as he drink then lie him

flat on the bed again. Rid sweat and shake and get angry and fret and do not sleep. He do not die neither. Howul must have save him.

#

As the sun show, Howul give Rid a different tea that push him into a most deep sleep and keep him in The Shapple all day. He tell Emlin he must again care for Rid who is still not Okay.

He then go to the tall grass by Rids house. He lift up the thick flat piece of wood and use the rope to climb down to where the plastycrates is take from. It is a long way down before hims feet touch concrete. He let go the rope and stand up. He have bring with him a oil lamp and light it. It show a cellar round him of People Before. Brick walls, concrete floor. Sour smell of stale water, mud, earth and soot.

On the floor is two long, straight lines of metal with thin pieces of wood between them. He do not know what they is for. Through a gap in a wall a narrow tunnel lead away from the cellar. The straight metal lines run through it. Howul walk between them, one wood piece at a time. He check what is in front in case of traps.

The tunnel is also brick. The smell is still bad and water drip in many places. The bricks curve above and beside like skin round hims finger. Why do they not fall on him? Will they crush him if he walk on? He want to turn back but want more to know where the tunnel and metal lines lead.

He get to a place where a big wood box with metal wheels rest on the metal lines. The box is big enough to carry all the plastycrates. When he lean over and look inside, he see the box is empty. Hims lean make it move forward on its wheels. Then it hit something. Howul fall off and graze hims knuckles. He wipe and lick but some blood drip onto the ground. He prefer if no one know he is here so wipe it up with hims robe. Many year of medicine have learn him that you bleed most long when you most want bleed to stop. And when you think it have stop it alway start again.

What the box have hit is a huge metal door. Its surface is flat except for a key hole big enough for a thumb to go through. Where is the key? And where do the door lead?

Anger at how long he bleed make Howul punch the side of the box with other hand. This also start to bleed. With both hands wrap in robe, he walk back along the tunnel and use the rope to climb up and out again onto the tall grass.

As he wait still for bleeds to stop, he sit cross leg and mind walk through place of herbishrubs and bumblybees. Then he go into Rids house. Perhap Rid have key. Inside is wood shelfs that shine and gleam, wood drawers, table, benches, a stool, plumpy cushions to sit on. Same as other small Big Houses except here nothing is on the shelfs nor in the drawers. Everything is in heaps on the floor. There is much to look through and he look through all of it. One huge heap is all bottles and tinfoods. Another is new make clothes – shirts and britches and three long blue robes he have never see Rid wear. Another is circles of metal all the same and each the size of a fingernail.

Next to this heap is a book very different to Jack and Julie Learn To Read and The A B C Book. The front and back is thin card. On the cover is a picture of a woman call Kelly. She is so real you can almost touch her long brown hair and soft brown skin. The shirt she wear is white and wet. It is too tight and her nipples push out against it but this do not seem to bother her. Inside is more pictures of women who also have clothes troubles. The red dress Christabell wear have lift up and show her arse. Debbies shirt have fall open and show her titties. Jane is in a stream of clear, clean water which have wash away all her clothes.

As well as what the girls names is, the book have other words. 'Bare is best', 'wild and wet', 'take me for a ride, big boy'.

Perhap Howul is wrong but he do not think Rid have this book to learn how to read.

After too long he put the book down and search everywhere for key. He do not find one but he do find a small piece of card with pictures on each side. One is of a huge grey building that reach into the sky like a fist. The other show a wide face, small blue eyes and a nose snotnoses can hide under. It is so sharp and clear it is like Rid himself stare back. What is the card for? Surely he can remember what he look like? Bad enough he have that face without put it on a card also.

When Howul get back to the room where he have leave Rid, hims new friend still sleep. He shake him till he wake up.

'Is you Okay?' he ask.

Rid lean over and vom all over the floor.

'No rest for the wicked,' say Howul.

Rid groan.

#

It is five day since Rid have any ganja or fly agaric. Hims face is more pink, hims eyes more clear but still Howul have tell him he must not move else poison may return. Howul use time to search for key in Rids home and in dell beside. He never find it. Now he save Rid and is so much good friend to him, he ask instead.

'Do you like keys?' he say.

'What?' say Rid.

'Keys. I like them. If anyone give me one, I keep it in my pocket. Is that good place? Where you keep yours?'

'I have no key.'

'If you do have, where will you keep it?'

'I do not have so I do not. Isnit?'

Perhap what Rid say is true. That Howul have return so oft and look so hard tell him he already have spend too long with Gold People. He need plan, purpose. Chop trees, footstamps and no hunger is no more enough.

'How you stay here so long, Rid?' he say.

'You say I must. You say I will die else.'

'Not in this room. In Tangrish.'

'Stay so long in Tangrish?'

Howul nod.

'I have no choice, isnit? I stay till they ask me back.'

'Who?'

'Mister Yorath. Jims.'

'They send you here?'

Rid take a moment to decide if he will tell Howul or no. He decide no.

"I is good now, isnit? I can leave this room?'

Howul check hims eyes, tongue, hair, hands, feet, get him to cough, get him to bend, get him to close eyes and stand up then open eyes again.

'All good,' say Howul. 'You can leave when you wish. But no more mushrooms.'

'For real?'

'Yes. Else you is sick again.'

'Fuck in a bucket. No more?'

'No more.'

'Fuck in a fuck bucket fuck. Without mushrooms and ganja I go mad here.'

Rid have spend the past five day on hims back without much move and have think he is about to die. If ever there is time he talk and share, then it is now. Howul try again.

'The Green, the storys, pigeon stew, keriss plumpy of Milani and Tris, sea salt you taste in the air, smell of lemon thyme, watch the waves,' say Howul. 'I miss Blanow. You also?'

'So why you here?'

'I behave bad. They throw me out.'

'They do not kill you?'

'I run away. Why you here?'

Rid squeeze hims little eyes tight and drop hims head so he can see more of Howul over hims nose.

'You think Blanow is only Blanow?'

'What you mean?'

'Where you think Blanow tinfoods is from? You think we make them in Blanow?'

'You mean tinfoods is from here?'

'Yes. No. It is complicate.'

The big blue plastycrates. The tunnel. The tinfoods Rid have in hims house. The huge metal door.

Billy bully work on Rid before to make him lie still for five day. Now he try again.

'Some people in Blanow say there is tunnel. And door. Is this how you get here?'

Rid open hims small eyes as wide as they go. Shock.

'No one say this. Who say this?'

'They say it at shite pond. They do not know I is near.'

'Who?'

Who is easy. Anyone in Blanow who is high up. And who Howul hate.

'Jims. Droo.'

'No one say this.'

Rid stand up. He know I give him billy bully, think Howul. Not so. It is just how Rid show angry.

'When I return, I make sure they is punish.'

'When you return?'

'Of course. I go back as Brenin when Mister Yorath die.'

Now Howul is not sure who billy bully who. He try again.

'They speak also of key to door.'

'The Big Keys? They talk of them?'

Big Keys. Big House. Big Drop. Big Tris. People in Blanow need more words.

Howul know now there is keys, not key.

'At shite pond, yes. And where keys is.'

'They say where keys is?'

'Yes.'

Rid now pace in small room and is ready to punch or smack something.

'Jims tell you he and Droo have Big Keys?'

'Yes. You is excite. I give you tea?'

'Tea can gofuck.'

More and more now fit. Jims and Droo have the keys for the tunnel that connect Blanow to Tangrish. Only Blanow can open and go through. Everyone in Tangrish call Howul Madbad as soon as they see him. He and Rid is not first Madbads they meet.

One thing else. Howul scape Blanow when they want to kill him. With tunnel, why they not come and kill him here now? Or take him back? They must not know he is here. Yet.

What Rid say next stay in Howuls mind as fix as grey in slate.

'Kimry decide all. Blanow is nothing without Kimry.'

Howul want to ask what is Kimry but Rid grab him, give him Gold People hug, say –

'You is not so shitebag, isnit?'

– and leave.

#

Howul find out what Kimry is more soon than he expect. This same night, the footstamps is even more loud and weird than before. Some shout and wave thems arms in the air as if attack by bumblybees. Others roll on the floor and scream as if on fire. Featherwoman spin round and round so quick that feathers fall off her and float through the air like dandelion heads. She stop and hold up her hands. After more shouts, screams, waves and rolls, everyone else notice, hold up thems hands and stop also.

'Let us give thanks,' she say.

She close her eyes. Everyone except Howul and Rid do the same. She give thanks for food, water, people, tools, electrics, trees etcetera etcetera.

As she finish, Steve walk in with someone Howul have never see before. He wear a long blue robe like the ones in Rids house. He is can hardly walk plumpy. Only a man who matter much can get so much food. A lucky man. With every slow step he pat the back of hims neck with a big green cloth. Everyone open thems eyes and hurry about him like scarify chickens. Some bring water, others potatos and spinach.

'Welcome back, Caddick,' say Featherwoman.

Caddick ignore her, wipe hims face and drop the green cloth on the floor.

'Old Brenin in Kimry is finish,' he say.

There is gaspings and oooings.

'New Brenin is Ista.'

More gaspings and oooings.

'New Brenin Ista say every crate must be fill complete. And he want more crates.'

Caddick sit down. Howul pick up the green cloth he drop and offer it to him.

'Bugger off,' he say.

Howul bugger off. Beth bring him a clean cloth. He wipe himself with it then drop it on the floor. This time Howul do not pick it up.

'When a crate is fill complete, much fall out,' say Featherwoman.

Caddick tcha and wave hims hand at Featherwoman like he push away rotted fruit.

'What new Brenin in Kimry want, new Brenin in Kimry get. Isnit?' he say.

He stand up again and slow step outside. Gold People follow. Eight animals Howul have never see before stand in a line. A rope tie them together. Everything of them is too big – too big faces, too big teeth, too big ears and much too big stomachs. Thick brown hair stick to them like marsh grass. Instead of feet they have hard round black stumps.

The one at front is most big face of all. He have two clothbags and a long metal tube on him. Next all have small blue plastycrates on them. The last in the line is the most small with most small face. Behind him a big wood box on wheels is tie to him by rope. In it is big plastycrates like the ones Howul have see Gold People take from Rids house.

Gold People take the crates off, put them down and replace them with others. Those they take off is fill with tinfoods, bottles and powder like the barley dust Big Tris use to make pattycakes. Those they put back is fill with knife handles, bows, arrows, wood plates and other wood items the Gold People make. As they do this, the animals heehor loud enough for the deaf and dead to hear them. Rid tell Howul they is call donkeys, is stupid and cack a lot.

More wood items is bring and cram in the blue plastycrates. Anyone can see that, as Featherwoman have say, much of what is in will fall out if the crates is move. Gold People know it but still smile as they cram. What Ista new Brenin in Kimry want, Ista new Brenin get. Even if he is shiteforbrain.

Caddick go over to the plastycrates the Gold People have take off the donkeys. He remove from them as many tinfoods as he can carry and put them in the two clothbags on front donkey. In plain sight, he steal. And no one seem to mind. Howul ask Rid where have Caddick come from and where he go now.

'Kimry,' say Rid.

'What is metal tube on donkey?'

'Gun. It hurt people.'

Steve put a wood step next to front donkey and hold tight the rope round hims neck. Caddick stand on the wood step and climb on donkeys back. Front donkey heehor. Caddick stab the side of hims head with a stick. He heehor again, shake hims head and spray snot over only person still close. Howul. Everyone else know to stand away.

'I can help you,' Howul say to Caddick. 'If anything drop out of a plastycrate I will put it back.'

'Gofuck, snot face.'

Caddick now stab front donkey in the stomach with hims

stick. Steve pull the rope forward. Nothing hap. More pulls, more stabs, many heehors, still nothing. Then, of a sudden, front donkey start to run. The other donkeys is pull forward by him. The big wood box roll forward too. Then front donkey stop. Other donkeys stop. Wood box still roll forward and hit back donkey. Knife handles, chair legs, chair seats and plates fall out. Howul pick them up and put each back where they have fall from.

'I keep them fill complete,' he call out to Caddick.

Caddick turn round, watch him then hold up hims hand, flat palm. Words is too much. Hims hand speak for him instead and also say Gofuck. Hims scowls, steal, hand speak and plumpy stomach all show how high up he is.

'I make sure new Brenin have what he ask for,' Howul call out.

'You want to go with him?' Steve ask Howul.

'Not want. Must. I have to leave. Urgent bizzy.'

Caddick is fed up that others talk, not him. He take the gun from front donkeys back and point it at Howul.

'You know what this is?'

Howul smile and nod like he have three of hims own.

'He is good Madbad,' Steve say to Caddick. 'Everything he do, he do good.'

The donkeys move forward three more steps and stop suddden again. Howul again pick up all that drop and put it back.

Caddick consider then say –

'You steal anything or run away, I blow your head off. Clear?'

Howul smile and nod again.

'You ride a donkey before?'

More smile and nod. More show what other want to see.

Caddick point to the back donkey. Howul climb on him. Hims top is make of rock and there is two blue plastycrates where Howuls legs want to be. Donkey heehor and drop cack out behind him then bite arse of donkey in front. The line move forward quick.

'Let us give thanks,' say Howul as front donkey lead them away from Tangrish.

#

JOURNEY

Deep water soon block thems way but Steve show them where it is shallow enough to go through. Some time he stop, stare at the sun, look round him then change where he lead them. The deep water spread far and wide but alway he know the way.

As items drop from the plastycrates, Howul fetch them from water and put back.

If they feel like it, the donkeys stop and do not move even when Caddick stab them with stick. They walk only when they want to walk.

When the sun is most high, Steve lead them up and beyond the water to dry earth, scrub and rocks. No trees, no birds, just piles of wood and dead fires. Steve put hims big arms round Howul, hug him and squeeze all breath out of him. Even if Howul have want to push him away, he cannot.

'May your journey be simple and safe, Howul,' he say.

He do not now hate Steve. He do not wish bad things to hap to Gold People in Tangrish same as hap to Gold People in Forse. He just need to be away from them. Footstamps, fill stomachs, warm clothes – all have soft thems minds. If he stay with them more, hims mind soft also. Or Blanow come for him.

Steve head back down to where the deep water is. Now it is just Howul, Caddick and donkeys. Front donkey stop again. Caddick smack hims face, smack hims arse, stab hims arse, stab hims stomach. He do not move. Caddick climb off and shout at Howul to take hims place. Howul climb on as Caddick squeeze hard front donkeys testicles. Donkey rush forward and pull the other donkeys with him. Caddick fall on the ground.

'Pull hims ears,' he shout.

Howul pull hims ears and front donkey stop so quick he throw Howul off. Donkey rush forward again. Howul grab the rope and pull. Donkey do not slow down so Howul run along next to him. Items scatter everywhere then, just as sudden as he have start, he stop again. The other donkeys and the wood box pile in to him from behind.

Howul now have donkeys and the gun. There is enough

food in the clothbags for him to live some day more. Caddick is far away and have only rocks and dirt and dust. Take over. Leave him. Move on? No. Too much is new. Who else can he learn from? How else will he know what hap when you pull a donkeys ears or squeeze hims testicles? And where can he go?

As Howul wait for Caddick to get to him, he pick up and put back what have fall from crates. At last Caddick arrive, hims face pink and drip with sweat and every breath a punish. He do not seem so big special high up now. He stand a moment then take a glass bottle from one clothbag and put it to hims lips. Then he pass it to Howul. No more scowl and gofuck. Like the Bells poison Mister Yorath have give him, this is a torch in hims throat. He swallow, gasp and pass it back.

When front donkey feel like it, they all move forward again.

The sun have fall low in the sky when they at last leave the dry earth and rocks behind. They walk along a shallow stream that bring them to a pond of clean water. The donkeys drink from it then go lie in dust. Caddick tie thems rope tight round a big willow then sit under it and torch hims throat again. Hims pink face is now beetroot red and he start to hiccup.

This annoy him. He stand up, hiccup, sit down, try to stand up, hiccup, sit back.

'Punch me,' he say and try to stand up again.

You do not need CURE OF EVERY FORM OF DISEASE to know a punch rid someone of hiccups. Howul help Caddick up then punch him hard in hims plumpy stomach. Big air rush from hims mouth. He stay quiet for a moment then stumble over to front donkey and take gun from hims back. He point it at Howul.

'Why you punch me?' he say.

Howul know the gun is dangerous but not how.

'To cure the hiccups. It work, isnit?' he say.

'I give you a chance. And this how you return me?'

Caddick drink from the bottle again but do not offer it to Howul.

'You is not here to hit me,' he say.

He point the gun at Howul again.

'Madbads is arse. All of you.'

He spit as he say it and scowl.

'Anything you want to say before you die?'

'What?'

'Is that all?'

All Howul can think to say is Why? That seem too little also. He say nothing. Hims mouth drop open and he stare at Caddick in amaze.

'Madbad arse,' say Caddick.

He drink again, puff out hims cheeks and point the gun again.

'Bang,' he shout.

Howul look for where he is hurt. He find nothing. Caddick laugh more loud than any donkey heehor.

'You think I mean it, isnit?'

Howul close hims mouth and try not to show how scare he is nor how piss off.

'You think I kill you, isnit?'

He laugh some more and drink again from the glass bottle.

Strange enough, now he have play this trick on him, Caddick seem to like him more. Now, every time he look at Howul, he laugh.

He put down the bottle, step away and pull back a small metal tongue that stick out under the gun.

'Bang,' he shout.

He pull some more and this time there is a noise of thunder. The donkeys heehor and try to run away but the rope stop them. The bottle is smash into many pieces. Caddick drop the gun, lose hims footings, roll over the glass and cut hims arms and face. He go to the pond, fall into it and let the the water clean away the blood. Howul bring comfrey leafs. Caddick put them in hims mouth.

'Push them against where it bleed,' say Howul.

Still Caddick chew them then stand up, pull up hims robe, lean back and piss in the pond. He shout 'Bang' again, laugh and fall over again.

When it get dark Howul and Caddick lie with each other and the donkeys to stay warm. The donkeys snore, fart and kick out thems legs but not as much as Caddick.

#

NOWHERE

In Blanow, Howul have no plan except to make life less bad for Jen and Erin and him. In Tangrish, he eat, breathe, sleep, miss Jen, miss Erin, want to dob Beth, try not to want to dob Beth and, above all, want to go back to Blanow and kill all slimefucks there.

Now with every few moments, different plans whisper at him, nudge him and tell him why they alone is what he must do. He must get Caddick to take him back to Tangrish so he can be safe and dull again as long as no Blanow people come to kill him. Or get back to Blanow so he can be strong and brave and hurt all those who have hurt Erin. Or stay as is and make best of where Caddick take him. Or get to Kimry where all is decide.

He know only one plan have sense just now but the others still whisper and make him feel bad for not do them.

They travel in fierce heat over bare rock hills. Without Caddick to find way through and donkeys to carry food and water, they die many time. The more far they travel, the more oft Caddick spend with bottle on lips and fog in brain. Now when Howul pick up what is drop, Caddick no more care if he put it back or drop it again.

After five more day the land grow more kind – low, flat and rich with streams and ponds. Of a sudden Caddick is fill with purpose and hurry. No donkey testicles is spare hims stab nor squeeze.

They reach a wall with sharp wire along the top and a big metal gate in the middle.

'Welcome to Nowhere,' he say.

Howul hold the donkey rope as Caddick take out a key. As he put it in the lock, the gate swing back already open. Behind it is a huge man in thick black padded clothes that cover all hims body. Top of hims head is also black padded. Over hims neck and chin is brown scars like honey fungus. A strange pink mess is where hims left ear should be.

'Here already?' Caddick say.

'All is change now Kimry have new Brenin,' say Padded Man.

He take off a padded glove, put two fingers in hims mouth

and make loud whistle.

Behind him, several wood buildings sit low and flat. Three men come from the one most near. Two of them also wear thick black padded clothes, the other – Morgan – a long blue robe like of Caddick. Hims grey hair is crop neat and close but hims grey beard reach hims chest. Over hims back is a gun like of Caddick. Each Padded Man carry a solid metal stick. They cannot all be just to kill rats and cockroaches.

'Why you here?' say Caddick to Morgan.

Morgan go over to the front donkey. He pull tinfoods out of Caddicks clothbags and throw them on the floor.

'These is not for you. Why you steal them?' he say.

'I steal no more than before,' say Caddick. 'Some is for you also. Take what you want, isnit?'

Morgan nod at no ear padded man. No Ear walk over to Caddick and smash hims metal stick against hims arm. Caddick cry out but do not try to stop him. Howul do not try neither. Watch, wait, stay stupid, stay safe.

After No Ear hit Caddick again, Morgan point at Howul.

'What?' he ask Caddick.

'Madbad. Good Madbad,' Caddick say. 'Take what you want. Take all of it. Why you do this?'

'New Brenin change everything. This is what hap now if you steal.'

'You steal, too,' say Caddick. 'You stop, I stop, isnit?'

He move hims arms up to protect hims face as No Ear hit him again. Soon they is so mash up he cannot lift them no more. They stay at hims sides as the metal stick crush cheek, lips, nose, eyes, mouth. He drop to hims knees and sob. Still No Ear do not stop.

Caddick do not beg. He do not complain. He let himself be hit till he roll onto floor and lie flat. In Nowhere as in Blanow, people accept what they is give even if it hurt. Even if they is as big special high up as Caddick. Most time Howul do same. Accept or walk away as another person accept.

Morgan walk over to Howul and stare close at hims eyes, as if he can see through them clear to what he think. Howul look away, to show he make no threat. He have not steal. He is good Madbad. Perhaps they will leave him alone.

Caddick is now sit up again, arms and face mash up and eyes too swell to open. He is most like too damage to take in any more of why they treat him like this but Morgan still want to tell him.

'New Brenin punish the bad, reward the good,' he say. 'This is new Kimry.'

Stay stupid. Accept. Let Caddick bleed. Except Howul have already see too many people die in Blanow. He do not want to watch Caddick die also.

He go over to him and use earth to dry hims blood. He do not dry much before No Ear pull him away.

'He need help else he die,' say Howul.

No Ear hit Howul hard two time with stick then hit Caddick again.

Another shiteforbrain bullyboy.

After they kill Caddick, for sure they must kill him. He should not be here. He need food, need water, bring disease, need help like People Outside in Blanow. For many day he have believe he is Sissypuss and cannot die. Now he is less sure. But still as before he is Howul, son of Garith, son of Nominus. He will not die fright nor defeat. He will die angry.

When Tall Nole kill People Outside in Blanow, they do not fight back because they is too shag, too weak. Not Howul.

He go over to No Ear, poke him so he turn round then punch as hard as he can into the pink mess where ear use to be.

The other Padded Men run at him. Metal sticks crash against hims head.

#

The room have no windows. He do not know what is night and what is day, how long he is here nor where here is. Not again, he think. Then sound of heehors reach him. Still in Nowhere. Every so oft a part of the door is push open and a pattycake and water is push through. A concrete floor is to lie on, a narrow concrete ledge to sit on, a stink hole to shite in.

From time to time the Padded Men come in with Morgan. The one with no ear Howul call No Ear. Another have big lips and is Big Lips. The other is a squishface ugly fuck and is Squishface Ugly Fuck. They is not please when Howul call them this.

Back in Kimry, perhap Morgan make snotnoses laugh and is kind to the old and weak. Here all Howul see is cold hard evil. Get is all that matter. How he get do not.

Morgan ask Howul of Blanow.

'How many people?'

or

'Is Blanow Brenin well like?'

or

'Why you leave?'

Howul never say. If he do, soon there will be nothing else they need from him. Every time he do not answer, Morgan get Padded Men to punch him, kick him or cook hims skin with candles. When they do this, oft time Morgan tell them they do it wrong and show them how. The way he show alway hurt much more.

All they know so far is what Caddick have tell them. Howul is good Madbad from Blanow. Punch, kick and cook have not work on him yet. This do not stop them try again. And again. And again.

Today Morgan is not here. The Padded Men bring Tegwin instead. A tall, thin woman in a long blue robe like Morgan and Caddick wear. Her head is cover with cloth.

Perhap five year less than Howul, she carry a blue clothbag, is clean and smell strong of lemon. The pink paint on her nails and black paint round her eyes say she want people to look at her. But the skin on her hands is deepblotch red and her eyes is swellup with disease. Her arms and legs is like puffballs.The cloth that cover her head? She lose her hair, think Howul.

'How they treat you?' she ask him. 'You have enough food?'

She smile as if they have fun together then close her mouth quick. Her breath stink like she have swallow a rotted corpse. She take some tinfood from the blue clothbag.

'Smelina?' she say.

Howul know it must be food so he nod. Tegwin hand the tin to No Ear who stab into it with a piece of metal like he wish it is Howuls face. She point at the Padded Men.

'If you is treat bad, tell me,' she say.

'I is treat bad,' he say.

'We can stop it.'

She quick smile again then put some of the tinfood on a spoon and hold it out for him to eat. It is sweet white mush.

Kicks and punches have give them no answers. Now they use mush instead.

'You is from Blanow?'

'When you let me free?'

'You help us, we help you. You is from Blanow?'

'Why you here?'

'We need you to help us. Then we set you free.'

'Why you need me to help you?'

'We have new Brenin. Ista. Things have change. You is from Blanow?'

'What is Blanow?'

'How many people is there in Blanow?'

'Why?'

She give Howul more mush like he is her snotnose.

'You miss Blanow? You wish you is back there?'

'Yes. No. Back where?'

Another quick smile then she take a small piece of card out of her clothbag and show it to him. On it is a picture of a huge grey building that reach into the sky like a fist. Same picture as he see on card in Rids house.

'This is Kimry, where we live. Everything is there. Tinfoods. Fresh water. Warm home. Warm clothes. If you help us, we take you there and give you everything you want. There is many things you want, isnit?'

Howul want to see Jen again. Hold her and lie with her.

He want to see hims daughter again. He want her never to have hungry nor be cold nor sick. He want her not to be dead. He want to be good father to her.

He want to punish those who have kill her.

He do not think Tegwin can give him these things.

'In Kimry everyone is safe,' she say.

Howul have spend many day in a concrete hole while Kimry people attack him, burn him and keep him in the dark. He trust her only as far as he can piss. He will not tell her what she want. But perhaps there is something else he can give her. Perhaps this will keep him live.

'How long you sick?' he say.

She step back and smile, as if to prove she is not sick.

'You have blight. I can heal you.'

'How many people is in Blanow?'

'It will take time but I will heal you. I will make medicine for you. If you do not have it, you will die. I will heal you.'

She smile again then take a red cloth from the pocket of her robe and wipe her mouth with it.

'Way you can help me is answer my questions,' she say.

'Then you will die. Soon. Many in Blanow have blight. I treat them. I save all of them.'

'You is from Blanow?'

'Where is Blanow?'

She sigh, put the tinfood back in her clothbag.

'Only reason you live is because you is from Blanow,' she say. 'Kimry know little of Blanow. New Brenin want to find out more.'

'Your teeth soon fall out. Everywhere hurt. Everywhere bleed. Then you die. I can help you,' he say.

'Think about what I say,' she say.

'You same,' he say, as she leave.

#

Kicks, punches, tinfood mush, now they have another way to make Howul tell. Slow hurt, not quick pain.

Padded Men have tie hims hands and feet together behind him with rope. He lie on hims stomach on the concrete ledge. If he move, the rope get more tight. For many hour, they leave him like this.

He try again what Jen learn him. He think of lemon thyme, comfrey, camomile, bumblybees, waves, trees. He picture how they look. He smell the flowers. He hear waves as they slap or crash against rocks.

Perhap if he do not do this he feel even more bad. But bumblybees and waves soon give way to wild anger. Anger that it hurt so much to move so little. Anger with Morgan and the Padded Men and Tegwin. Anger with himself that he is here. Anger even with Jen and her stupid smell the flowers gobbledybollocks. The anger at last wear out and hims mind become empty, cold.

This time, Tegwin come in alone. Perhap they think he will say more this way. She offer him a spoon of mush. He ask her to hold hims head so the rope do not pull as he swallow. She gentle hold hims head and feed him. Then talk most quiet to him.

'Sorry they treat you like this. It is not what I want.'

'Soon you will die. Why you help them?'

'Like you, I have no choice. They make me do this. But please do not tell them I say this. How many people is in Blanow?'

He have not see anyone treat her bad. She is not tie up and leave on concrete next to a stink hole.

'What you mean no choice?'

She put her finger to lips then shake her head, like already she say too much. Or else it is all billy bully. For one time, Howul do not know which.

'Where you bleed from now?' he ask.

She give him more mush.

'Why you leave Blanow? Will more leave Blanow soon?'

'You think you will not die?'

'Just tell me. Please.'

'Where is Caddick? They have kill him, isnit?'

'Yes, they kill him. Help me else next they kill you. What sort of weapons is in Blanow?'

'You do not help Caddick. You do not help me. You help them.'

She put away the spoon.

'I cannot defeat them, isnit.'

They sit silent for a time, all words brack.

No Ear come into the room. The no noise make him think Howul have kill her. By stare at her too hard perhaps. By breathe at her too strong. No Ear seem disappoint she still stand.

She move over to the door to leave with him. And then of a sudden it start. Streams of blood pour from her mouth and nose. She take out red cloth and wipe her face. Still the blood pour from her. No Ear look away as if this will stop it hap.

'Lean your head back,' say Howul.

She do this. Still more and more blood.

'I can save her if you let me help her,' he tell No Ear.

No Ears brain fill with fuddle and fear. He do not move.

'Do what he say fucksake,' she shout at him.

No Ear cut through the rope with a small knife and free Howul. Howul push her head back and squeeze the top of her nose hard.

'She need salt water,' he say.

'Get it,' she say.

No Ear soon return with Morgan and salt water. Howul get her to drink some and spit it out. Most that return is blood. He push her head back again as he press on the bleed. He taste the salt water.

'It need much more salt,' he say and give it back to No Ear.

'She will live?' say Morgan.

Just as he say it, the bleed stop.

'She will now I have stop the bleed,' say Howul. 'Next I will heal her. I can make special potch for her.'

He do not know if she will heal or why the bleed have stop. But, if she do live, he is miracle man and perhaps they let him live, too.

They is still freak by what hap to her so when he ask for vegetables to give her Morgan say Yes. Way to heat them? Morgan again say Yes. Carrots? Spinach? Onions? Marigold flowers? Lemon? Dandelion? More he ask for, more it seem he know what he do. No Ear bring all of it.

The cooker is of thin metal with flame from oil burner to give out heat. Howul put on it a cookpot they have fill with water.

'The vegetables must be cut up,' he say.

No Ear take out hims knife and cut a carrot into pieces.

'Wrong shape,' Howul say.

He try again. Howul shake hims head. No Ear press knife against top of carrot and move it till Howul nod. He cut.

'Good,' Howul say.

They do the same again. No Ear cut. Howul hold up, examine piece of carrot and tcha.

'Wrong,' he say.

He talk carrots but think of the knife, the flame, the hot water.

'You do your best,' he say to No Ear, 'but it is not easy to get right. It take me a year.'

Morgan tcha and give him the knife. He cut the vegetables into many strange shapes then drop them in hot water.

He know the bleed may soon start again and the heal fail. He look for chance to scape or attack. But the knife and flame is too small. The cookpot is too heavy to lift and throw hot water from. And Morgan and No Ear stand too far back.

When all is cook enough, he blow out flame. He add cut up

marigold flowers and juice crush from the dandelion roots. The smell of them is of life and health and goodness. He add juice squeeze from the lemon. When everything have cool he mash it together with hims fist then put it in wood bowl.

'This will heal me?' Tegwin say.

'Yes,' say Howul. 'Yes, it will heal you.'

'It is just vegetables.'

Howul shake hims head.

'How you eat it make it medicine. Chew every piece forty time else it may not work.'

'It is just vegetables.'

If she do not believe him, no one will. He think of something else may help. In the pocket of hims green Tangrish robe is the pouch with keepsakes and teeny books inside. He feel for hims fathers keepsake – the teeny bottle of medicine. He take it out.

'The potch is not finish,' he say.

He add some drops to the mash. They have sit in the bottle perhap twenty year.

'What is the drops?' say Tegwin.

'Yellow campion. My best medicine. With it, this potch will heal you for sure.'

She put her fingers in the bowl, scoop out some potch and eat. It taste bad so she know it is good.

#

Tegwins hands is pink again, her eyes clear. Arms and legs good shape again. She do not bleed. Whatever her blight is, potch help mend it. Howul is healer. Miracle man. For the moment, safe. He think.

They have move him to a room with daylight, blanket and soft bed. The door is still lock but no more is he tie up with rope. Plumpy candles give him long light. Hands free and alone, he can write. What hap since he leave Tangrish. What they do to Caddick. What they do to him. He put it in few words so, more late on, he can remember what hap and add much more. Howul tell me all is for true but I do not have how Morgan say it nor No Ear. If I have, I do not think Morgan say he is cold hard evil nor No Ear that he is shiteforbrain bullyboy.

The door unlock. Howul hide the teeny book and pencil under blanket as No Ear let Tegwin in.

She sit down next to him on the soft bed. Again they is alone. She pat hims knee and smile at him. A cloth still cover her head but her breath is now free from corpses. She squeeze hims knee.

'You have help me. You save me. This is my thanks.'

She sit more close, press against him, kiss warm breath into hims ear.

It is long since anyone make play for him.

He want her. Only people who touch him recent is with punch, burn or kick. She stroke hims cheek with her fingertips then kiss where she have stroke. He do not stop her so next she kiss hims lips. Straightway hims heart melt, hims hurt mind ease. He kiss her back. A long sweet kiss, best since Jen. Only kiss since Jen.

He move hims lips away so they can both breathe again. She push her fingers through hims long hair. They kiss again then hold each other a long while with no words. All pain fall away from him. So much glad squeeze tears from him. He turn hims face away to hide them. She see them, stroke hims face and kiss each tear. She hold hims hand.

"Tell me of Blanow and I make all else good for you also," she say.

And everything is brack again. A gentle, kind, soft, warm kiss, fill with love. Then words that throw ice water over him. He still want her but not like this.

She take hims hand. He pull it away.

'No,' he say.

Before, whatever he do, alway she is sweet and calm with him. Now her face is scrunch up in anger, her quiet voice as harsh as any shout.

'Why the fuck you save me?' she say. 'If you do not answer the questions, we both die. Give me answers else Morgan kill us both.'

Her kiss then her anger unlock something in him, make him think again about what she ask for. If he give answers and it somehow hurt Blanow, why should he care? He want to hurt Blanow. All there hate him. If they kill him after he tell and they hurt Blanow, still it is worth do. He stay quiet but Tegwin sense change.

'Every new Brenin have something new,' she say. 'Istas is that he want to learn about Blanow. You tell me, I tell Morgan and he tell Ista. This way he can please new Brenin. Else you is dead already, isnit?'

'Why do new Brenin want to learn about Blanow?'

'They do not tell me.'

'Why you think?'

'If I know I tell you. I have not the foggyrest.'

She take hims hand again. This time he let her.

'I wish I can save you, Howul. I cannot. Morgan do not believe you will tell me anything. I hear him tell others he plan to kill both of us today. If you tell me of Blanow, at least I can live.'

She kiss hims hand, give it back to him, begin to weep.

'I must live,' she say. 'I must get back to Kimry. Please help me. I must see my children again. You have children?'

He flinch like she throw something at him.

'Help me,' she say.

In Blanow, bad things is simple. Here, Howul have think he is safe because he is miracle man who heal Tegwin. But if he do not tell of Blanow, he will die today. If he do tell, still he die but Tegwin is safe. And Morgan can please new Brenin. If all she say is true.

Howul prefer Blanow simple bad things.

'If I help you, I is finish.'

'You is finish anyway.'

'You have children?'

'Yes. Brian. Glin. Mary.'

She stop and blow her nose on red cloth.

'You will help?'

#

Howul soon find that Tegwin know as much of Blanow as he know of Kimry. He tell her of wet, smoke-fill caves where all Madbads live. The fish spears they use to kill People Outside. How clothes is for the weak so most time they is naked. The one hand stomach rub use by pregnens Madbads to make baby come out. The finger up nose to make rain stop. The drink your own piss and clean your face and hands with it. It please him how much gobbledybollocks she believe.

Whatever stupid things he pretend Madbads say or do, she accept all of them. She laugh at idiot Madbads and, in secret, he laugh at her.

Now he help her, Morgan and the Padded Men seem to forget how they treat him before. They even let him out of hims room but only if Tegwin or No Ear is with him and only into the next room. The floor and ceiling of it is white, the walls blood red. Paint, he hope. It is fill with tables, benches and shelfs with blue plastycrates on all of them. A heavy wood door to outside is lock.

Every day No Ear, Big Lips and Squishface Ugly Fuck empty big plastycrates of knifes, spoons, bows, arrows, plates etcetera etcetera then put them back in small plastycrates so one crate is all knifes, another all spoons etcetera etcetera.

Every day Howul make potch on a table by the only window in the room. Padded Men as well as Tegwin now eat it. It heal her so they think it will help them also. Big Lips think he now sleep more and can carry more. Squishface Ugly Fuck think he breathe less heavy and run more fast. No Ear think hims ear start to grow back. Miracle mans miracle food.

Through the small window Howul see the other low flat Nowhere buildings. One is where they keep the donkeys at night. Others is where Padded Men, Tegwin and Morgan sleep. Howul never see anyone else here.

Today as he wait for the vegetables he have cook to cool, No Ear and Tegwin is with him. As per the usual, the door outside is lock. After Howul mash them, No Ear slop some of the new cook vegetables into hims hands and rub this into the pink mess on the side of hims head. No Ear do not like the taste so do this with it instead. Still it work well for him, he think. Tegwin prefer to eat hers. Soon she will ask him again of Blanow.

No more Sissypuss, he is now Sherrysad – woman who must tell Brenin good new story every night else in morning he kill her. He still have plenty more gobbledybollocks to say about Blanow but hims fathers medicine is near finish. Soon there is no more potch. He show No Ear and Tegwin the bottle.

'I need more yellow campion to make this,' he say.

'You can get some?' Tegwin ask No Ear.

'What is?' he say.

'It is flower I use to make your ear good.'

He pour spinach and custard tinfoods onto white floor to show them how yellow campion look.

'Search for it under brambles, rocks, stones,' he say. 'The more hard a place is to reach, the more it like to hide there.'

No Ear leave and go find some. Tegwin ask of Blanow and Howul tell her of invisibilly bird which make thin Seesyseesysee cry but no one ever see and of invisibilly flower which you can see but which, if you eat, no one else see you.

She seem please with what he say so he ask her of Morgan and Padded Men and Caddick.

'In every while, Caddick take tinfoods from Kimry to other place then come back here with wood items.'

She look through window to make sure no one is near.

'Before they all steal. Here is fill with plenty they should not have. Morgan steal much more than Caddick. And now Morgan kill him so all can be blame on him.'

'You is alway here too?'

She look through window again.

'New Brenin Ista send me here to watch Morgan and see how much he have steal. Morgan know this and look for way to kill me. With you he find it. When he return to Kimry, he can say you kill me. But first he must know of Blanow.'

Kimry is like potch. All is so mash and mix up is hard to know what anything is.

No Ear return with mint, nettle, lettuce, yucca, fern, fennel, clematis, comfrey. Wrong smell, wrong leafs, wrong shape, wrong size, wrong taste, wrong colour.

#

Next day other Padded Men help No Ear go find also. No Ear bring more wrong flowers to Howul than anyone. Anything that grow, he bring. Howul say No to all. Till No Ear smile and pull a flower from under the padding on hims wrist. A keriss, simple flower with five petals which neat divide in two. He give it to Howul.

'Yes, this is campion,' say Howul.

No Ear is as please as if hims ear have already full grow back.

'You see a problem?' say Howul.

No Ear do not so Howul ask Big Lips.

'Perhap it have lose its colour?' he say.

The petals of the flower is white.

'White campion is not yellow campion,' say Howul.

The door open and Morgan come through. Most time he leave Howul alone. Tegwin tell him what Howul tell her. He have no need to hear for himself.

He throw Howul a look as sharp as rats teeth. This is it, think Howul. I have think I is safe and now this is where he kill me. The potch and Blanow billy bully have help keep him live but now time is run out.

Morgan reach into hims robe. Howul expect him to take out a knife. But Morgan have see that, since Padded Men have potch, they all work much more hard and much more long and there is never complain. He do not want potch to end yet. He do not take out knife. He take out a small yellow flower.

'I see this by the stream when I wash,' he say.

The flower is one they have not find before.

'Yellow campion?'

Howul take it from him, smell it, pinch it.

'Sorrel,' he say. 'And see this.'

He hold the medicine bottle uppity down over the cook vegetables. When he shake it, no drops come out. He try again. Still none. Then at last one slow drop fall.

'Near finish,' he say.

The Padded Men look at Morgan, wait for him to tell them what to do. He point to a big plastycrate still fill with wood items.

'Empty them then we all go look,' he say.

#

A rope round thems waists tie No Ear and Howul together. When No Ear pull, Howul follow. Much like donkeys except less noise. No Ear lead Howul out of the big room to a metal gate. The gate where Howul have first meet him. Still it is unlock. The clean air taste as good to Howul as cool stream water.

They go through the gate to the flat land beyond. Morgan, Tegwin, Big Lips and Squishface Ugly Fuck wait for them there. Together they will search for best medicine flower.

'No doubt you look hard before, isnit,' say Howul. 'But, remember, it hide under things. It try for you not to find it.'

'Show us where,' say Morgan.

'Here is too dry. It need to be more near to water.'

Instead of pull Howul, No Ear now let Howul lead him. They walk till Howul find a muddy pond with rocks and a few trees by it.

'They already search here,' say Morgan.

'It like to hide,' say Howul. 'May I?'

Morgan let him. The others watch as he search slow and move each rock away so he can see any plants beneath. He bend down to get more close to one. As he do this, the rope become tight and jerk him back.

'We must do together,' he say.

As Howul bend down, No Ear bend with him. Howul pick and hold up a shy yellow flower with flat pale green leafs.

'Purslane,' he say.

The sun hide face behind clouds. Rain then hail throw itself on them like it do not want them to be there, like it want to keep the yellow campion safe. Everyone is soak. Everyone suffer.

Howul move on to a circle of rocks with a thicket of brambles inside. Other plants hide under or push through them. He kneel down to see them more good. No Ear kneel also. Morgan, Tegwin, Big Lips and Squishface Ugly Fuck come over to see what they find.

'May I perhap have more light, perhap?' say Howul.

To be extra polite will, he hope, annoy Morgan more and make him think less sharp than if he just do simple ask.

The others step back to make more light. The hail still beat on them so all want this over quick.

Perhaps you think Howul have big plan in all this. Not so. He just know that, lock up all day, he have no chance for scape. Outside may give chance.

The Padded Men is all big men. Since they no more torture Howul, since hims potch make them even more strong, they treat him like favourite idiot Sky in Forse. They laugh at hims thin arms, skinbone chest, no muscules. To them he is weak. But none have never see him run. He run most fast of all in Blanow. This give him hope.

'There,' he say. 'There it is.'

No Ear look where Howul point then look back at him.

'Yellow campion. Under the brambles. Right there. You see it?'

No Ear do not. He push hims head forward and get more close. Still not.

'Yellow. Under the brambles. Perfect. You see?'

No Ear look ahead, look back at Howul, look ahead again. Nothing.

'See? It like to hide,' say Howul. 'I need a stick to reach it. May I?'

He get up and hold out hims hand for No Ears metal stick. No Ear offer it but Morgan stop him.

'Of course. I understand,' say Howul. 'It scare you if I have it. Sorry I ask.'

Nothing scare Morgan. Not least thin arm no chest Howul. He take the stick from No Ear and hand it over.

It is thick, strong, heavy. Like No Ear.

'I can show you it more easy if we is not tie,' say Howul.

The hail hail. The ground mud. All is grump and cold.

Morgan give Howul death face but still get No Ear to free him.

'Where is it?' say Morgan.

'Yes.'

'Where?'

'Oh, sorry. There.'

He push some of the brambles back with stick and point to where he have just search. Everyone look where he point.

'I cannot see it,' say No Ear.

Too stupid even for this, think Morgan. Hail, mud and cold have make him rash. He push No Ear out of the way and kneel down to look for himself. As he do this, hims gun roll off hims shoulder and onto the ground. Quick as a scald lizard, Howul smash him over the head with the stick and grab the gun. He want to run but No Ear now come at him. Howul point gun and fire. The end of it punch into hims shoulder and push him back hard. No Ear fall down, twitch and groan.

Morgan hold the back of hims head and try to get up from the maze of brambles he is in. He reach for hims gun and see that Howul have it. Hims mouth drop and he watch amaze as Howul fire again. He clutch hims stomach and collapse into brambles.

Big Lips and Squishface Ugly Fuck see all this and is not sure if to rush him or run. They check with each other, nod and rush. They slip in mud and stumble. Howul fire at them both.

Everything hap in a blink. There is no plan. He just do. But still he is not finish. All round him is blood and groans and crush, brack men. He go to No Ear, press the gun to hims chest and fire again. No Ear lie still.

Hims ribs and shoulder is hurt by every punch from the gun. He do not fire it more but use No Ears metal stick instead. It is same as when he mend brack bones or clean wounds. He feel nothing. He just do what he must till everything is best he can make it. When he heal people, they scream with pain and beg him to stop. Same now as he kill them. He carry on till all of them is still, quiet, dead.

When he is snotnose, only reason he live is because he is more old than hims brothers. If he have die one of them live instead. He do not die so both is put in Field of Black. Now he piss on death again. Lucky unlucky Sissypuss Sherrysad. The one lemon thyme seed from hundreds that is not eat by insects nor blow into the sea nor rot in the earth. Why him? Still he understand this no more well than can a lemon thyme seed.

The hail stop. The sun return. Tegwin have watch everything without move. She stand now with hunch shoulders and bow head, as if this make her disappear. It do not. As Howul look at her, she begin to tremble.

He wipe the stick on the soft ground to remove the blood. He cannot see there is blood all over hims face and in hims hair.

Tegwin hunch her shoulders again as he go over to her.

'I wont tell anyone anything,' she say. 'You have my word.'

He think what to do. All is fog.

'If I let you go, you go back to Kimry?'

'I will say they kill each other because you scape and they argue the blame. Please.'

If she go, he is never safe. If he kill her, he is as bad as them. He do not want to kill her. He want her to hold him again.

'You have children?'

'Yes. Three. Brian. Ted. Mary.'

'When you last see them?'

'When I leave to come here. They do not want me to go.'

They both stare at the ground then look up, catch eyes, look away. All at same time, like bird dance. They wait. They do not move. The silence hurt both of them. Then at last she speak.

'You make it up, isnit?'

'What?'

'Yellow campion. There is no yellow campion. Isnit?'

They fall into silence again. After what seem many year she begin to edge away from him. Edge, edge then brisk walk. He watch her go. A wide, flat path lead from the pond away over more flat land.

Of a sudden a thinking hit him. Brian. Ted. Mary. Brian. Ted. Mary. First time he ask her about her children, they is Brian, Glin, Mary. Now is Brian, Ted, Mary.

No one forget the names of thems children. Yellow campion isnt all that is make up.

He can still see her. The flat land stretch without feature except one big rock. He watch as she reach it and walk in its shade. He brisk walk after her. It do not take him long to get close. She hear him and know straightway why he is here. She begin to run. He chase after. She stop.

Because hims right shoulder hurt, he use hims left hand to pull her back toward him. Her face is close, her breath sweet, her skin soft and warm. She do not move nor struggle as he stand behind her, put metal stick over her neck and squeeze breath from her.

She lie to him about children. Is all else make up also? If she get back, all Kimry come after him. This is why he must do it. He close hims eyes and squeeze more tight. And see again Jen when he find her after cyclone then Erin in cave then hims brothers and son that is take from him. He think of noises Padded Men and Morgan make as he kill them. Sobs fill him. He drop metal stick.

'Sorry,' he say. 'Sorry.'

First he want to kill her. Then he want to save her. Crazy Madbad. She pull away from him, shoulders hunch, head bow. She cannot look at him.

'Sorry,' he say again and walk away.

#

Some of Howuls story is what he write near the time of it, some he write or tell me more late on. As I say before, I do not know what is true, what billy bully. But with Tegwin, all is sharp and clear as if he watch it hap as he tell it. Of what hap straight after he remember little. At some time he return to Nowhere. He say he go first to the building where the donkeys is keep in at night. He think they will have tire of inside and want to come out. They see state of him and stay where they is.

He go next into the room with blood red walls and start to chop vegetables for potch. He do not think clear as he do this. He do not want potch, he just want something to do. One moment he miss and chop table instead. Knife stick in table. As he pull it out, he lift too high and slash hims chin. It bleed like fuckery and of course do not stop. Lucky unlucky. All these people he kill and first big bleed he get is one he give himself.

The red walls of this room is hard for him to look at so he go next to the room with the daylight and soft bed. Hims Tangrish green robe is now more hole, tear, mud, stink, blood and home for insects than cloth. He put all on the floor and leave it. For him, for now, naked seem right.

He open pouch and take book and pencil from it. He look for words to write but other words get in the way. Hims brain is a fire. Some time the smoke is so thick that he can see nothing. Some time what he see is so bright and blaze so fierce that he do not dare write it.

He reach for pocket to put pouch in and remember he is naked. As before, he now keep pouch in place by wind snake skin round it in hims hair. He lie down. Hims heart pump loud and wont let him sleep. He get up and go outside. Stones and pebbles begin to speak to him. He pick them up and throw them away so he wont hear what they say to him but, as soon as he do this, other stones and pebbles speak.

'You kill them,' they say. 'You kill them.'

The donkeys is outside now. They sit in the mud and dust and do not move, like to be inside for so long have weary them. Howul walk gentle over to them and lie down beside them. They keep out everything for him except breathe and snort, breathe and snort till sleep at last hold him.

#

JOURNEY

He follow the footprints in the dusty earth back to where he have leave them. Red kites now pluck and scratch at the bodies and flies cover them. He look for something to hide them with. Plants perhap. Or put them in pond. He try to move them but hims shoulder still hurt too much from the gun and hims chin start to bleed again. With this and mess from the dead, all hims body is like he have wash it with blood.

He go to where last is Tegwin. He do not find her. The path she have take is wide and flat with no mud nor big holes nor loose rocks nor stones. It is best he have ever walk on. He follow it till at last the land get bizzy again with gorse and brambles and small stumpy trees, a steep hill and a stream. He drink from it and move on.

As dark fall, the path go round a village of scrag fall down houses and one good house with walls and roof. Howul think the dark will hide him but a man hear him and walk over. He wear a red People Before hat and red People Before coat. Brenin, think Howul.

He do not call for anyone so Howul suppose he do not mean to have him kill just yet. Instead, Brenin lead him to the good house. Its windows have corrygate iron over them so no light can get in. The door is two tall pieces of corrygate iron that reach up to the roof. A big chain can hold them together but is unlock. Brenin move one piece to let Howul in and close it after. Inside, oil lamps throw light onto tinfoods and glass bottles on shelfs and a door through to another room. Rest of room is dark. The house have walls and roof but is small and shite compare with Mister Yoraths.

'Here is Madbad,' say Brenin.

Why he say this to me? think Howul. Then he realise he speak to someone else in dark of room. She step into the light. Tegwin.

Before her is a tall, codfish ugly, stark bollocky naked Madbad with blood all over him. Who not long before have try to kill her. But who also have heal her and spare her.

'All is Okay,' she say to Brenin. 'I know him.'

And that is all. She do not say how she know him. Nor how

115

he kill people. Nor how, if Kimry have find out who he kill, it want him dead. Not yet.

Brenin open some tinfoods and bottles of beer and hand them to Howul. The tinfoods is all white.

'Only the best,' say Brenin then leave them and go in other room.

The walk have weary Howul but he do not want food. He want Tegwin to understand.

'You lie to me. You have no children.'

'I try to save myself. You do same. Now we must help each other and trust each other. Else we both die.'

There is beds in room for them both. Perhaps she wait till I sleep then she have me kill, he think. He is by now so shag that even this thinking do not keep him from straightway fall into sleep.

#

Hims bark shoes have long since fall apart and he have walk here with bare feet. Brenin have notice and next day bring new, strong bark shoes for him to wear. He put them on. They fit well. Brenin also bring bucket of water for wash. As he do this, he notice how much blood he have on him. It turn all the water red. Now he is with Tegwin, he wish he have clothes as well as shoes. Brenin bring for him a dark green robe like he have in Tangrish. With pocket for pouch. Next he bring condense milk tinfoods for them. When they finish he pull open corrygate to let them out. Tegwin give him circles of metal same as Howul see in Rids house.

Tinfoods. Bottles. Welcome. Bed. Shoes. The blue robe she wear and the circles she have make Tegwin special. With them, village Brenin make fuss of her and Howul. Same in next village and next and next. Where she go he follow.

Apart from Brenins, everyone else in villages keep out of thems way and look bizzy. Naked snotnoses with huge eyes and sunk stomachs, growups with bone for chest, sticks for legs and thick rope for veins. They pick and pull and dig and plant and weed, pile wood, make clothes, carry water in jugs.

Howul see but feel and say nothing. At least when Jen die he have Erin to care for. When Erin die he rage at what they do to her. Now there is nothing. He eat white tinfoods that smell of metal. He drink beer and burp. He see weary, half starve people work till thems hands bleed. He see thems snotnoses bite and suck on twigs and pretend this feed them. He take what is give him then walk on. Only thing that reach him is what stones and pebbles shout at him.

'You kill Gommel. You kill Morgan. You kill Padded Men. You let your daughter die.'

Only way to stop them is move on.

#

KIMRY

More day, more villages. Stones is more quiet now. Tegwin have try some time to talk to him but give up when she get no answers. Now she try again.

'See that?' she say.

Of course he see it. Far ahead is a tall mud wall. Beyond it, through clouds of thick grey smoke, a huge grey building reach into the sky like a fist. Much more than a village. Much more than Blanow or Tangrish.

'Kimry,' she say.

She take hims hand and squeeze it. He have not expect this. He have almost dob her and almost kill her but still he know her little. Perhap now is time to start. He search hims mind for something interesting to ask her.

'You like Kimry?' he say.

She seem please that he speak and what he say make her laugh. He is not sure why.

'You will see how Kimry is,' she say. 'Some things is good.'

'You have no children. You have a man?'

'No.'

'Woman?'

'No.'

She do not say it like she want to say more and already he have speak more than in all the past five day. But now they speak again there is one more thing he have for her.

'You will say in Kimry I have kill Morgan and Padded Men?'

She squeeze hims hand again.

No,' she say. 'I will say they fight over how to share what they have steal. Fight and kill each other.'

A heavy wood gate fill the only gap in the mud wall. Two Padded Men stand outside it as they reach it. Both carry metal sticks.

'Madbad?' one ask Tegwin.

'Good Madbad,' she say. 'He is with me.'

They open the gate and Howul and Tegwin go through.

They reach another heavy wood gate where more Padded Men wait. Again they is let through.

The path now wriggle past houses with rotted wood roofs and fall down walls. Thick smoke rest in the air above them. Behind them ditchs lead to shite ponds where red kites screech and scratch. The air taste bad.

There is no men here, only skinbone women and snotnoses. They move slow like thems arms and legs is too heavy for them. All wear dusty muddy red rags that stretch from neck to knees. The smoke smudge with black thems hair, faces, arms and legs.

The houses stop. Now there is noise of shout, scream, smash, hammer and clang. On one side of the higgurdy path is a deep trench fill with water then the huge grey building that reach into the sky like a fist.

On the other side is many deep pits. In the first Howul can see men and boy teen skinbones in red rags. They throw wood onto flames that burn under big clay boxes. Piles of bricks is here also.

In the next pit is more flames, more big clay boxes, more skinbones. Glass shapes is stack up here, some small as a hand, some large as a door.

In the next, skinbones pour redhot liquids through white flames into huge stone troughs. Bricks. Glass. Now metals.

Next, different kinds of high stink mess – old food, old clothes, dead plants, dead creatures, dead people. Skinbones set fire to them. The smell is so bad that Howul and Tegwin breathe light and move on quick.

In other pits is make charcoal, concrete, weapons, chairs, cushions. Only thing not make is clean air. Round the top of every pit is Padded Men with metal sticks.

A old skinbone in one pit is cover in soot with bright red burns on face and arms. He is alone and bash at hot metal with a hammer. Every bash is like he try to kill the metal, not shape it. Tegwin point at him.

'Griff,' she say. 'He use to be Kimry Brenin.'

In another is twenty naked skinbone snotnoses. They sit crossleg on dry earth. None move nor speak. Most old have perhap eleven year but is so skinbone that her face is old womans. By them is a woman in red rags and with shave head. She have a baby at her breast. Even the baby is skinbone with purple mark on neck and back, like deep bruise. Men with sticks to guard twenty snotnoses, a woman and a baby. What bad thing can they do that need this?

The smoke stay deep in Howuls throat. No swallow nor spit out can rid it.

Tegwin lead them to where a thick piece of wood cross the trench of water. A wood gate is on the other side with Padded Men by it. Everywhere in Kimry these men watch, wait, say little, do little, look fierce. As Tegwin and Howul walk over the piece of wood, the men mutter. Madbads is not every day for them.

So many noises and people. And everything so big. Pits, Padded Men, the huge grey building. Even the gates.

She speak to a Padded Man then come back for Howul. Together they go through the wood gate to open ground in the shadow of high stone walls. More Padded Men join them as they move across and through a small wood door and into a narrow tunnel light by candles. It smell of smoke, damp and roses and lead into a room more big than any Howul see before. It have many doors. Padded Men is at all of them.

The old floor is of hard white stone which still shine no matter how many feet have walk over it. The high walls is of wood and is light by red and yellow electrics. On them is signs of People Before. What is Toilet? Buffet? Sauna?

'What is this place?' Howul ask Tegwin.

'Great Hall,' she say.

Close to them tables is pile high with food on glass plates. White liquids full of maggot lumps. Thick yellow slop. Sticky brown dollops. Apart from soft white pattycakes the size of fists, all is tinfoods and most is white tinfoods because, as everyone say, these is most clean and most good.

Other tables is pile high with items. Lamps, cookpots, cushions, blankets, knifes. Blue robe people pick up and look at them. Some they keep and put circles of metal on table for them. Those not by these tables loll in soft chairs and goss with each other.

Skinbones in red rags bring and clear food and drink. All have bare shave heads, big sweat smells, sharp edges, sunk stomachs, stick legs and stick arms. As Tegwin and Howul go by, skinbones drop heads and blue robe people stare.

Near sign that say Clock Tower a door lead off. More Padded Men is by it than any other door. Again they let Tegwin and Howul through. Now is a room with eight walls and no windows, cramp and tall at same time. The floor is cold bare white stone.

'Room of State,' say Tegwin.

Along each wall, candles sit on pieces of metal and throw light onto pictures of strange animal with big teeth and long knifes that stick out of top of hims head. Each wall and picture is a different colour. Red wall have red picture of strange animal, yellow yellow etcetera etcetera.

Pictures is low on walls because much of room is stone stairs. These round and rise up more and more high to door at top.

A hallooshanin now approach them. A man in a long blue robe with close crop neat grey hair and a grey beard that reach hims chest. Morgan.

He step toward them. Left side of hims face move but right side now do not. Same with left arm and right. He cough as he try to say something and use a white cloth to catch flem.

Every part of Howul shake. The man he have kill now stand before him, brack but live.

'Where is others?' Morgan ask Tegwin.

'I must speak to Ista,' she say.

'Where is Morgan?' Morgan ask Tegwin.

This do not seem strange to her but she do not want to give him answer. He stand in her way till she do.

'I must tell Ista.'

'You must tell me.'

Still he do not move.

'Dead,' she say. 'All of them. Morgan also.'

When he hear he is dead, Morgan make sad choke noises in hims throat.

'I wish it were not so but it is.'

Morgan look at Howul like he have never see him before. Perhaps the attack have not kill him, only what he remember. Forget Howul, forget he is Morgan. He move close to Howul, stare him hard.

'This Madbad kill them?' he say.

'No. I tell all to Ista,' she say.

Morgan let her past and in line they go up many many steps. They go slow because one half of Morgan keep try to stop other half from move.

And now Howul work it out.

In Blanow, only one twin can live. The other is take to Field of Black. Here in Kimry, twins can grow to full age. Brack flem man is Morgans twin.

Through door at top of steps is a long dark room. Thick carpet cover the floor. Over this, two lines of candles show where to walk.

At the far end is a black cloth door. Morgans twin pull it open and go through. Tegwin and Howul wait. Padded Men watch Howul like any moment he will try to blow out a candle or attack them with one.

After some time Morgans twin come out and wave for them to join him. A small square room with a spiders web light same as in Mister Yoraths house and Tangrish. It is so bright it take Howul a moment to see good again. Thick carpet cover the floor here also. Two walls have big circle windows. Other two have pictures of poppys, anemones, roses, jasmines, foxgloves and tulips. They look more real than real flowers. On floor is metal wheels of different size with metal wrap round them like rope.

A strong smell hit Howul. Not flowers but lemon and rotted flesh. In the middle of the room is a tall wood chair which is turn away so he cannot see if anyone is in it. A thin, high noise arrive from behind it.

'Show us,' it squeak.

Morgans twin bring Howul and Tegwin forward to other side of chair. In it is a person with the same ill as Tegwin have before. Green blankets is over hims legs. Round hims collapse chest is a red jacket with thick lumps of yellow metal on each shoulder. The back of the chair rise so high behind him he look like a snotnose who sit where he should not. Hims skin is so white that veins stand out on it like pencil marks. Hims blood red eyes sink back deep into hims bloat face. He have no hair and big red mess cover hims cheek and nose. He is skinbone and bloat at the same time — hims neck twig thin, hims fingers and legs plumpy as if fill with water. Hims chest rise and fall quick as if he have just run up hill.

Tegwin start to speak then stop. She have not expect him to be like this. She cannot look at him.

Ista. A near death man. The new Brenin everyone is so scare of, everyone try so hard to please.

There is blood in hims mouth and round hims teeth. Hims breath smell of corpse.

Hims teeny red eyes stare out at Howul from hims plumpy face.

'You is Madbad?' he say.

'He can tell you of Blanow,' say Tegwin. 'Thats why I bring him.'

If she expect thanks, she do not get any.

'Loyd tell us Morgan is dead,' say Ista.

Loyd is name of Morgans twin. Again Tegwin start to speak and again cannot.

Howul have see enough ugly sick people to know what is for true. When you look at them, they prefer if you do not seem shock and about to upchuck. He stare at Ista like blood, blotch and bloat is normal to him.

He have see how much Kimry have, how much it make and take. As in Blanow, life must be more easy for those Brenin favour. If he can please this new Brenin, anything he want may be hims. And any billy bully he make up about Morgan is more like to be believe also. Trouble is, right now Ista is three breaths short of expire.

'I can tell you much of Blanow,' Howul say. 'First this. Many in Blanow have same blight as you. I heal them. I can heal you.'

Istas shoulders drop and hims eyes blink something away. Not water – blood. He hold up hims redblotch hands.

'You promise what everyone promise,' he say. 'Everyone in Kimry say they can heal us.'

Tegwin have not tell Ista yet how Morgan have die. So Howul do it for her. But different.

'Morgan die of what you have,' he say. 'And others also. All is dead when I arrive. Tegwin have it also but I treat her and she live. Isnit?'

'He heal you?' say Ista.

If she wish, Tegwin now can say what have hap for true. She do not wish.

'Yes,' she say. 'Others is dead of it and he heal me.'

'How?'

'With special potch.'

'Loyd say he must cut us with knife to let out blood. Some say only cure is not eat. Now you say eat special potch. You is all full of it.'

'It work for me,' say Tegwin.

'What is in potch?'

'Vegetables,' she say.

'Fucksake.'

He look at Loyd like he is ready to send them away.

'And this,' say Howul.

He reach into pouch for teeny medicine bottle of hims father, take it out and show Ista.

'From Blanow. No one here have this.'

'You have this?' Ista ask Loyd.

Loyd take bottle, look at it.

'What is?' say Loyd.

'Extract of yellow campion,' say Howul.

Loyd give bottle back to Howul.

'It make no sense to take this,' he tell Ista.

Howul hear Tegwin breathe sharp next to him. He open the bottle, squeeze some drops onto hims hand, sniff it then offer it for Ista to sniff.

'I add it to special potch. It heal in Blanow. It heal Tegwin. It save you also.'

Ista lean forward and sniff. Hims nose so stream with blood he will not smell shite in a shite bucket. He will not know that, since the drops run out, the bottle is fill with water. Howul decide he will not tell Ista yet he must chew potch forty time. Way hims teeth is now, one chew is too many.

'It do no good?' Ista ask Loyd.

'No,' say Loyd. 'None at all.'

Somehow this help Ista decide.

'Look at us,' he say to Tegwin.

She lift her head, gulp, look.

'If what you say now is lie, you is finish. Not just pits. Finish finish. You get?'

She nod.

'So. You is ill same way?'

'Yes.'

'And this help you? Save you?'

'For sure. For sure.'

Howul offer hims hand again for Ista to smell. He wave Howul away and say this to Loyd.

'We is most sad for what hap to Morgan. He is most good

brother to you. And alway great help to Kimry.'

It may be hims pain and bleed as he speak but it sound to Howul like Ista mean flip of what he say. Sad is glad. Good is bad. And why do he say We? Is he so sick he do not know there is just one of him?

Ista close hims eyes and go quiet. Sleep? think Howul. Die? No. It is what all Brenins do. Keep everyone wait to show how high up they is. At last he open hims eyes again.

'Very well,' he say. 'Start now.'

So far, all is good. No one here except Tegwin know what hap in Nowhere. No one try to kill him yet. Perhep here he can start again.

#

Next to Ista, Morgan and Loyd is most high up people in Kimry. After they speak to Ista, Loyd want to know more of how hims brother die. He stop Tegwin and Howul in eight wall room and ask this.

'All of us is ill together,' say Tegwin. 'We try to help each other but is no good.'

'Help each other?'

'For sure.'

'Morgan know you is only there to watch him. He tell me this before he leave. But still he help you?'

'When people is sick they is different,' say Howul.

'I know how sick people is,' say Loyd.

Howul think he speak of himself but Tegwin say –

'Loyd is medicine man also.'

'What of Caddick?' say Loyd. 'He die same way?'

As Howul see before, bad things in Kimry is never simple. Already they have give Loyd plenty of billy bully. Mind can only hold so much. So now Tegwin go for true.

'Your brother kill him,' she say. 'He say he is thief and kill him.'

'Sound like Morgan,' say Loyd.

There is still more he want from them.

'You think you can heal Ista?'

'Yes,' say Howul. 'For real it work on Tegwin. I have try to save your brother also but already he is too much ill.'

'Before, most people here is in the pink. Now more and

126

more is sick same way.'

'In the pink?'

'It is phrase.'

'Many have it in Blanow before I cure it.'

'What you think cause it? Ista think it is poison but he is away with the furries.'

'Furries?'

'Phrase. Some think bad air or bad mud or bad clothing bring it. What you think, medicine man?'

Howul have mend Tegwin but have no idea how nor what make her ill. Simple time keep people simple. Now we all read again everyone know what then they do not. Eat vegetables and there is no blight. Some high up Kimry people only eat white tinfoods. For long, only Brenins can eat them and only of rare time. Then many more is find in Kimry. Everyone agree they is best and want to eat them to show how high up they is. Simple people.

'Bad air, mud, clothes is to be avoid,' Howul say. 'Or perhap it is bring by birds.'

'Alway we have birds but only now this blight. You sure you can mend Ista?'

'You is medicine man. You know there is no sure. What you think bring blight?'

'Perhap we do not see for look. Nose on face, isnit?'

'Nose?'

'Phrase.'

#

After ten day Istas eyes is less red, hims skin less blotch, hims voice more strong. Blood still clag hims mouth but he live. He can move again. The potch Howul have make for him plus the miracle drops have help him.

Howul also tell him plenty of Blanow. Same dribble as he give Tegwin. Madbads live in caves, kill People Outside with spears, go naked, drink piss etcetera etcetera. He use burn end of spark stick and scratch on floor to show Ista what Madbad in Blanow look like.

He tell Ista how he scape from Blanow by swim for two day then reach Nowhere by follow trail of donkey plop. Ista seem to believe all of it. He even give Howul a blue robe to wear. In the pocket is a small piece of card with picture of huge grey building on the front and cod fish ugly face on the back. Long, thick black hair with snake skin tie round it. Howuls hair. Howuls face.

Blue robe people is call Kings People. Howul is Kings People now.

They is in the small square room with the flower pictures. Ista have send others away so they can speak alone. Again he sit in the tall wood chair. Again he wear the red jacket with thick lumps of yellow metal on each shoulder. Under it is a blue shirt with small bones and string which tie it across hims chest. The jacket is huffy but the shirt is baby soft and smell of rosemary. Hims britches is grey lines with teeny white lines between. All hims clothes is People Before, of course.

Howul hope to please Ista by heal him and tell him of

Blanow. Blanow gobbledybollocks please him but not heal. He grump about how bitter potch is and why, when he eat so much, he do not heal more quick. When Howul say he must chew forty time for this, it grump him even more.

Howul know from hims father that not all people you heal is please. Some time they hate person who heal them for be more well than them. Some time they get angry because they is shame to need help. Some time they is so weak that angry is only way they can still show strong. Some time they is just arsepain grumpscrut. Ista is arsepain grumpscrut. He not only grump about heal. He grump about everything. So do Howul, of course. Howul wonder if hims grumps annoy others as much as Istas grumps annoy him. He decide not. He know he only grump when he have good reason. Ista grump for sake of grump.

What he grump about most is other Kings People.

'Thiefs, devils and bumsucks,' he say. 'Grabby, greedy, gormless. Dangerous. Spoil. Sick in head. We give them white tinfoods and still they moan. Loyd and Morgan is most bad of all. We is well rid of Morgan. It is good he is worm food. We wish Loyd is also.'

Every place he is, there is alway a Brenin everyone else puff up and lie to. Alway another high up the Brenin pretend to like but hate and fear. Alway some stupid headcrusher who do as Brenin tell. Perhap it is same as water is alway wet and nettles alway sting. Then he think of Gold People in Tangrish. All there is Gold. Why?

Ista is not some shiteforbrain village Brenin. He is above everyone. So in square room he sit and make Howul stand.

'All want me dead,' he say. 'All want to be Brenin. Is it same in Blanow?'

When he is in Blanow, Howul never want this. He never think what Mister Yorath have can be for him and no more want to be him than he want to be red kite or fish. He do not want what cannot be. He do not say this. He say instead what he think Ista like to hear.

'In Blanow, everyone want to be Brenin also,' he say. 'Brenin make life easy for them but still they want more.'

'How people is, isnit? They expect new Brenin to do more for them. When you last have new Brenin in Blanow?'

'Not for many year.'

'Your Brenin is lucky, isnit?'

Plenty for Howul in Kimry is still fuddle and fudge. For instance why do Blanow matter so much to Ista? Tegwin say it is way to make new Brenin special but Howul know there is more. So he ask.

'I tell you much of how Blanow is. What is reason you want this?'

When people speak to Ista, most time they creep, cringe and If I May Dare to him. Howul throw this question straight. He scowl first then soft. It make a change for him. Also it give him chance to talk about what he love most. Himself.

'As new Brenin we show we can do what no Brenin do before. We go to Blanow, take Blanow and make it Kimry. We show all those bumsucks and shitebags here who is best.'

Ista carry on with more talk of how bad hims life is and how everyone else is blame for it. If I share with you all he say it will bore you as much as it bore Howul. So I tell you instead of where Howul take hims mind to as he pretend to listen.

How, after Ista make Blanow Kimry, Howul will kill all high ups there who have kill hims daughter. How life is for high ups in Kimry. How Kings People do not cut nor carry wood nor fish nor make bricks nor bash metal but most time loll and feed and drink and sleep and get red rag skinbones to do things for them. How still thems lifes is not easy because they forever worry about what Ista think of them. How they fear to upset him and be punish and send to pits or, as he say to Tegwin, be 'finish finish' by him. How, if they ignore him, this might upset him. How, if he notice them, this might upset him more.

Ista get up from hims seat. Howul decide to listen again.

'Come with us,' say Ista. 'We show you how bumsuck they all is.'

They go to the eight wall room Kings People call Room of State. Oft time only Ista and Loyd and Tegwin and other most high ups is here. But it is also room some come to who have fall out with others and want to hurt them by tell Ista bad things about them. They think Ista will like them for do this.

First who speak now is a grooly man who say keriss woman have say she want more big home when home she have is plenty.

'You want more big home?' Ista ask her.

'If I may so dare, I never say this. For true my home is plenty, if it please you.'

'So why he say you say it?'

'He have creep me by keep say how keriss I is and I have tell him to stop.'

'You do not like he say you is keriss?'

'I do not like where he try to put hand as he say it.'

A old man want young man punish for call Ista cunt.

'You call us cunt?' say Ista.

'No,' say the young man. 'I mis-say or he mis-hear. I say Ista cannot do more for us than he already do because already he do so much. I mis-say or he mis-hear cannot. He know this but is annoy with me for not be more good son to him.'

'He is your son?' Ista ask old man.

'He insult you,' say old man. 'He call you cunt.'

Another say someone else have take flysticks from him without ask.

'You take hims flysticks without ask?'

'No. I ask and he say I can take.'

'So why he say different?'

'Because he do not have any when he need them and is then bite by moskits.'

Ista decide who he believe more. That person then spend more time in eight wall room. Other person keep head down and keep away or some time is send to pits.

Last today is two men about same age of Tegwin.

'If I may so dare, my wish is to speak to you about water,' first say.

'Speak,' say Ista. 'We will listen.'

'This man blame you for have no clean water, if I may so dare,' he say.

'You say this?' say Ista.

And now something different hap. The other man admit.

'If I may, yes. I have no clean water,' he say.

First man speak again.

'He say Griff have promise this.'

'You say this?'

'If I may, yes. Griff have promise this.'

Last Brenin Griff now bash at hot metal in pit, cover in soot and with bright red burns on face and arms.

'You want Griff back?'

'No.'

'But you want clean water?'

'If it please you, yes.'

'How is the water not clean?'

'It smell of metal and run brown, isnit.'

'Brown, you say?'

'Yes.'

'So you is a man with water that is not clean?'

'For sure, if it please you.'

'So how clean is your face?'

'My face?'

'Your face is not clean?'

The man have shiny clean face and shiny clean hands.

'I get clean water from others.'

'Griff have promise you clean water for wash?'

'Yes.'

'Have we promise you clean water for wash?'

The man sweat and fidget.

'No,' he say. 'Sorry to trouble.'

'It is not trouble,' say Ista. 'Clean water to drink is not enough. Clean water to wash will be yours also.'

'Thank you.'

'Every time you wash you will remember us.'

'For sure. It is most kind.'

Everyone know but no one say it. Only place this man wash soon is in a pit.

As Ista tell all what he do about big house, cunt, flysticks and water, most bow heads and listen hard. They show respect. They let him know he is above. But not Loyd. He pull face, tcha and grump as Ista talk. Now Ista push back. He point to shiny face man and say –

'Arrange clean water for him, Loyd, and all others who want it. When things is bad, alway we make them good.'

Like two snakes in a circle, they hiss at each other but never strike to kill.

#

Kimry is big place with many, many people. Scores of Kings People, hundreds of Padded Men, hundreds more red rag skinbones. When somewhere is so big it is easy for things to be lose. And people. Huge grey sky reach building have many rooms and is where all Kings People live. No one have tell Howul any rooms is hims but Tegwin let him share with her. How kind to help him. Except he know she only do it so she know where he is, what he do and who he speak to. Also she have space. Her home is five big rooms with carpet on floors, dry petals that fill everywhere with scent of roses, pink candles that share scent of lavender as they burn and oil lamps that give light by day and night. She prefer them to electrics.

In the most quiet room is a bed for Tegwin as soft as a babys cheek. No man, no children, just her. In the most big room is a huge black chair of People Before, also just for her. Pieces of wood stick out from it. Pull one and it lean back. Pull another and it is a bed. Tegwin never pull them, never light candles, never fill lamps with oil. Alway there is red rag skinbones to do this for her.

If she ask for a table, chair, dish, plate, glass, cushions, tinfoods, straightway they is bring to her by skinbones. Vegetables. Fresh water. Warm clothes.

Howul ask Tegwin about them.

'They is punish for do bad things,' she say. 'We call them scanks.'

They must do many bad things because there is many, many scanks. Also, most must have do bad things young. Only old scank Howul have see so far is last Brenin, Griff.

For most of hims life, Howul scrape and struggle. Much more is take from him than give him. Now he can have all he want. He know that, if he ask for anything, a scank bring it. He wish he do not have to ask and can just go get instead.

Tegwin is not bother. As she and Howul talk now in her home, one scank squeeze her toesys and another rub her feet. Both say nothing and keep thems faces blank. Tegwins toesys and feet is keriss but Howul prefer if it is him that squeeze and rub them and not scanks.

Most time they is out of home in Great Hall or Room of State or Howul is with Ista in flower pictures room to give him potch and hear him grump. But end of each day they is here. He talk plenty because this mean he stay more long with her. He like how she look and smell. Do she talk plenty back? No. She close off. He find it hard to know what she think or mean or feel of anything. Alway there is delay before she speak so she can stop whats real from show. Oft time in Nowhere she is same. But there also he have see her angry and fright and desperate.

He try now to scratch and scrape out more than she of usual give.

'Why you have no man, Teg?' he say. 'Why no child?'

She point for scank to squeeze next toe before smile at him and say –

'It is complicate. I tell you other time.'

This is how she is. Hear, smile and not give back.

'Why not tell me now?'

She smile again.

'There is much here you still do not understand. It is not your blame. That is how it is till you is here more long. When there is more understand, I tell you more.'

'So much have hap already before we is here. Tell me now.'

Another smile as she point for scanks to leave them.

'Why you want to know?' she say.

'Most time with people, I watch, wait, listen, say little. With you, it is different. What have hap have change that.'

'How?'

He try to unlock her. Instead she unlock him.

Guns is simple compare with words. Words is guns, clodges, spears, cyclones, knifes, fires, feathers, kisses, mind walks, pattycakes, diseases, rivers, leafs. Some seem one thing then is another. Soothe then hurt or hurt then soothe.

In Nowhere Howul see Tegwin as enemy and block her. Here in Kimry it is different. She get him to say what else he do not. As now. He cannot stop himself. He tell her for true what he feel.

'I care about you, isnit?'

She look back at him like he is interesting moss on rock or animal she have not see before. He wait long while before she speak.

'You is good man,' she say. 'You spare me. But you is right. We go through too much. We think we will die. We almost die. You also have bad sleep?'

Even in soft bed with warm blankets he now sleep more bad than ever before on stone floor. He nod hims head. She take hims hand and give him stare like fish eyes.

'I care for you too, Howul. That is why you stay here. But we help each other. Nothing more.'

She give him back hims hand. As oft time with her, it is only when he have her answer he know what it is he have ask. For him to be her man. And she have say No. There is no Challenge in Kimry. Instead there is ask and answer. It is complicate.

#

Even though half of Loyd is brack and he cannot speak without cough, dribble and spit flem, he is still the main go-to person for Kings People when they is sick. Because Howuls potch have heal Ista and Tegwin, others now want it also. Loyd do not like this.

The big room they is both in have no carpets and only two chairs. The floor and ceiling is concrete. White paint on the walls have peel away to show more concrete. It is a room that do not want to be look at nor come to. Loyd have choose it.

Behind Howul is a grey concrete shelf. On it is glass bottles of medicines of People Before that Loyd use. Howul put here the potch he have bring. As they begin to treat and heal, he see that few people here have Blanow diseases. No sweet piss. Stiffneck. Gangrene. Some have same blight as Ista. And, like in Blanow, some pretend more bad disease for themselfs. A bruise is a brack. A cough is lung fail. A sneeze is fever and certain death without quick help.

A skinbone call Ivor bring them water and pattycakes and look more ill than many of them. Only twelve year, perhap. Hims thin body stretch up as if every second he grow more tall. Hims thin face is so stretch back it make hims nose look size of a fist. He smile plenty, help some to walk, listen, bring. He seem for real to care. And never let this drop. And, because he is skinbone red rags scank, no one except Howul ever notice.

Loyd decide who they will look at next.

'All work no play,' he say.

A woman of perhap twenty year make many loud noises of pain. She stare at them with big wet eyes. Loyd nod at her and she walk up to him like each step almost kill her. Ivor help her.

'What hurt you, Trinny?' say Loyd.

'It hurt when I sit down,' she say.

Loyd get her to turn round then lift up the back of her blue robe. Her arse have a huge red lump on it.

'You is in the wars,' say Loyd.

'She is not in the wars,' Howul say. 'She have boil.'

'She know what I mean. Isnit, Trinny?'

Trinny smile as Loyd pat and squeeze round where the lump is. He then pull the robe down over it again and get Ivor to bring a brown medicine bottle from the concrete shelf. Loyd shake from it a small white tablet and give it to her.

'This will put hair on chest, Trinny,' he say.

'Why you put hair on her chest?'

Loyd ignore him. The phrases show everyone how high up and special he is.

Trinny swallow the tablet.

'Be brave soldier and see me again tomorrow.'

After give Loyd a circle of metal size of a fingernail, Trinny look at Howul.

'Can I have Ista potch?'

Loyd tcha as Ivor get some for her.

'It is just vegetables,' he say.

Trinny screw up her face as she swallow some then walk slow away with more noises of pain.

Next is a young man with near death blight. Already he have no teeth nor hair. Hims arms and legs is bloat and each foot is size of two normal. Hims breath would kill cockroaches. He is with a young woman who help him walk.

'You make good progress, Moxy,' Loyd say. 'Soon you will be in the pink.'

'Tablets you give me is no good,' Near Death Moxy say.

'It take time,' say Loyd. 'Home isnt build in a day.'

'I do not have time,' he say.

Moxy look at Howul.

'You heal Brenin?'

'Yes.'

'Give me what you give him.'

Ivor bring potch. Moxy stare at it like it is more bad than hims disease.

'This is scank food,' he say. 'What you give Brenin?'

'This.'

He pour some in hims mouth and spit it out like it is mud and cack.

'No Brenin ever eat this,' he say.

'Let it be,' say Loyd. 'Let us try this instead.'

He take out a small sharp knife.

'It will save me?' say Moxy.

'Most sure.'

He press the knife against Moxys right thumb. Blood drip out slow and thick.

'Be strong. Be well. Come back tomorrow.'

Moxy give Loyd a circle of metal.

'It still bleed,' he say and show how blood from hims thumb drip to the floor.

'That mean it work,' say Loyd. 'Soon you is fit in a fiddle'

The young woman lead him away but return not too much time after. She sit on the ground and wait as they treat others for boil, bloat, blotch, blight etcetera etcetera. When they have all leave, she stand up and walk over to Loyd and Howul, steps slow and heavy.

'How is your brave soldier, Catrin?' say Loyd.

She ignore him and speak to Howul.

'You have more scank food I can take to him?' she ask.

Howul get Ivor to put potch in a dish for her.

'You think he will eat it?' say Howul.

'If I give it to him,' she say.

'Potch do no good,' say Loyd. 'What he need is less blood. He have too much.'

Loyd know all Kings People names and say them plenty so they think he care. But true is he do not. With hims half brack body he think he suffer more than any of them. Any bad they have is what they bring on themselfs. Howul ask how he decide which tablets to give.

'They get what they get,' he say. 'Buggers cannot be choosers.'

True is he have no idea what is in them nor what they do.

When Howul hold hand of sick and dying, splash water on thems weary brows and say kind words, most time he feel no more than when he take off shoe or wash plate. But he still want them to be well again. He notice that Catrin have not leave yet.

'What you need?' he say.

'I have ache that never go,' she say.

'What you need now is rest, Catrin,' say Loyd. 'Come back tomorrow.'

He drag hims brack body away.

'Where is ache?' say Howul.

'My head. Even with close eyes it still push and press inside.'

This is why Loyd leave, think Howul. She have a case of the mentals.

'The potch will help your man,' he say. 'You have some also. Perhaps then you feel more good.'

'Before Moxy get sick I lose my baby. He die of cough.'

In Blanow many mothers lose thems babys. Some die of disease, some is take from them to Field of Black. Howul speak to her like he speak to them. He ask her hims name. Where he lie now. What she like best of him. She try to answer then stop.

He remember white season when he have eight year. The sun hide, ice fill the air and the earth is cold hard rock. Jims and Droo have just take hims new brother to Field of Black. He sit with father and mother on The Green in the sharp cold and say nothing. Hims mother have same dead eyes, dead face as Catrin have now.

New brother is with them two season before they take him from them.

'The earth will be a gentle blanket for him,' Howuls father say. 'Do not be sad. He is safe now. Peace is with him, Howul.'

Hims mother hear nothing, say nothing. She stand up and walk back toward thems house. Hims father brack off a piece of pattycake and give it to him. It taste of wood crumbs. He try to swallow but cannot. Hims first brother he have want to die. Perhaps this is why they kill hims second. To punish him.

When they return home, hims mother is not there. They search and search but after many day still cannot find her.

White season become green season become gold become brown.

When white season start again, Jerry discover her as he cut wood near Big Drop. Her bangle of shells is round a bleach white wrist bone.

Ivor help Howul lead Catrin from the room. They grip her

138

arms and move her up steps and along passages light with blue electrics. She hold dish of potch tight to her and try hard not to spill any. Howul tell her there is more but she do not seem to hear.

At last they reach door to her room in the huge grey building. She open it and go in. Howul follow.

The room smell of disease. A huge bed is by one wall. Pile on top is empty white tinfoods and glass bottles. On the floor under some blankets is a bald naked man with bloat arms and legs. Moxy. The man who have spit out the potch. Her man.

She lie down on floor next to him, stroke him and hold hims dead hand.

#

As in Blanow, people in Kimry think books is bad. No one read nor write because they is too bizzy with eat white tinfoods and drink beer. Howul think perhap Loyd have a book with the phrases he use but he never see anyone else read or write. So he is surprise when he ask scanks to bring him books and they bring three. The green front of one is all mess up and goopy. Inside is more goop and mess and pages not there. The words on the pages which is there is all gobbledybollocks for instance –

"Vivamus mea Lesbia, atque amemus,
    rumoresque senum severiorum
    omnes unius aestimemus assis."

Some time there is a word like Die or Me or Dare but with nothing nearby to join up in sense with. On many pages every word is strange.

The next book is also weird, but different weird. The words look normal but still make no sense for instance –

"Punters hoping for a good turn out at Haydock Park
    should make a beeline there on July 24th. Expect no
    plodders and plenty of promise in this exciting
    afternoon's racing on the flat. Blanket finishes
    aplenty, we predict."

Perhap People Before use different words. When we might say 'lots of blankets is throw away' perhap they say 'blanket finishes aplenty'. Perhap plodder is sort of man. Sick man. Old man. Tall man. Perhap.

The front of the next is as usual mess up and goopy. On it in big black letters is these words –

"BEDDGELERT, BLAENAU FFESTINIOG
CHWILOG, CRICCIETH, CROESOR
DEINIOLEN, DINORWIG, DOLBENMAEN"

He do not know any of these words. Even the words in the words – BED, A, IN, LOG, OR – is no help. Many of the pages inside is also mess up or not there. Those that is there have crisscross lines with more strange words inside them – Fron Fawr, Tai Taliesyn, Towyn Rd, Dorvil St, School, Library.

The more he know of People Before, the more easy it is for him to see why they is no more. Even though they have so much, most of what they write is gobbledybollocks. In a strange Howul way, this please him and make him try more hard to keep hims own words straight and true. He keep the three books but not all the pages in them. Any that is blank he rip out so he can write on them when all hims teeny books is fill up. He fill up more now as he write of Kimry and Ista and Loyd and home with five rooms.

Some things he still cannot write. How the Padded Men groan and scream and beg as he kill them. How hard the gun push against hims ribs and shoulder. Tegwin as she edge then walk away. Hunch shoulders. Sweet breath. Warm skin.

#

The two snakes circle in the Room of State. Many high ups is here. Ista have sort out man who say another man have steal shirt from him, woman who say another woman have poison her food and a woman who say a man say Ista have cock size of peapod. Now Loyd speak.

'Your friends miss you,' he say.

Ista have no friends. No one know what he mean.

'We have so many friends it is difficult to please all of

them,' say Ista. 'Which friends miss us?'

'In the Great Hall. They wonder why you never go there.'

True it is he never do this. He prefer hims flower pictures room. Even Room of State is pain to him.

'Tell them we will visit soon. We wish we have more time for them. But alway there is so much bizzy as we make things more good for them. Tell them that.'

'They want to thank you for all this good you do.'

'It is kind but we do not do this for thanks. We do this for them. You will tell them this.'

'So you will not tell them yourself? Many think you hide from them.'

'If they think this, they is not my friends.'

'So you will not go to Great Hall?'

'We have say.'

'They say you is too pissypants to go there. Too yelly belly. They say if I ask you and you say No, it prove this.'

Clever Loyd. Challenge. Test. Make Ista look weak whatever he say or do back. Anyone else is straight in the pits but Ista know Loyd is too strong.

'Very well. We will go there now.'

Great Hall is like The Green in Blanow. Where people go for goss and food. In Blanow only the goss never run out. Here food never run out neither. Ista walk now with Loyd, Howul, Tegwin and other high ups. As he pass Kings People that loll, he throw empty words at them.

'Life treat you well?'

'All good?'

'No troubles, we hope?'

He wait as they answer. Most is too relax to say much to him and none is stupid enough to complain of troubles. Instead they say how kind and clever he is and what great Brenin he make. He listen careful, say he just do hims best and tell them they must come see him if there is anything or anyone they is not please with. It all make Howul want to vom but is like when someone have bad shakes. You want them to stop but cannot keep eyes off.

Now everyone look at Howul as if he is special also. Even if he wish, he can no more keep low and avoid. It feel strange but good.

Two young women stand up as Ista go by. One have black hair, one yellow hair and both is Caddick plumpy. You cannot tell where head finish and neck begin nor same with stomach and legs. How men want all women to be. Soft. Warm. Keriss. Ripe. Except, with these two, all they is ripe with is anger. Thems eyes spit this at Ista. He walk past them without stop.

'Hattie and Jessie. Daughters of Griff,' Tegwin tell Howul.

Great Hall have many parts to it. In one is space with three walls like separate room but open. On the walls is big sharp pictures of People Before. They have huge faces where you may see every lump and bite and scratch except every face here is pink and smooth and clean. All smile with gleam white, no brack, no black, no gap teeth.

Under these pictures is a green table. People stand either end with thick wood plates in thems hands. They use them to hit dry, round puffballs at each other. A mesh like a fisher net split the table in two. One person hit a puffball onto table. It bounce over mesh and other person hit it back. This excite them so much they groan or shriek or jump up and down like thems testicles is on fire. They shout out numbers as they do so. It is a game.

As Ista get near, one offer wood plate to him. He take it and start to play. Shout out numbers change every time white puffball hit ground or mesh. People come over to watch Ista. They cheer when he do anything at all.

For Howul, the game last as long as it take water to freeze in gold season and is as thrill to watch. The other person is more young and strong than Ista but oft time drop wood plate or hit puffball into mesh. On purpose, of course.

'You is too good for me,' he say.

Another step forward and take wood plate. The Griff daughter with the yellow hair. Till now only men have play.

'Enough,' say Ista and give Howul wood plate.

'Too scare?' say Yellow Hair.

She hit puffball hard onto table. It bounce over mesh and up toward Istas face. He knock it away with hims hand. The other daughter is behind him and walk fast toward him. Howul see that she hold a long knife. As she stab, he put wood plate in way so she stab it instead. It break but stop knife from reach Istas back.

Padded Men run over, grab daughters and drag them off as they scream at Ista and promise him more hurt for what he do to thems father.

Istas leg shake as he say –

'We is well. All is good.'

He answer a question no one have ask.

#

Scank have bring Howul one more book. It have no front nor back. The pages is yellow fade. Some words make no sense to him. Metaphysics. Philosophy. Chariot. But many do make sense and, when he read it again, some become more clear because of others round them. Nightingale is Bird. Ivory is White. Student is Shiteforbrain.

I have not see this book nor read story as he get it. All I have is how he tell story himself. Before he change it perhaps much is different. Everything good, everyone happy like in Jack and Julie. As per the usual, in hims story bad win and good is crush. Do not trust anyone, it say. Beware billy bully.

He only write words that make sense to him. No metaphysics. No chariot. He say it how he want to.

ROSE

Boy tell girl of love.

'Mine is more strong than iron,' he say. 'More deep than sky. More shure than truth.'

She smile. Brite eyes spark.

'How can I win yoo?' he say.

'Bring me red rose,' she say.

Nex where he live is garden with red rose tree. But cold erth have stop tree from grow. No leef nor flower, only bare brantchurs, thorns.

He sertch else where. Every where. He find wite roses, yello roses but no red. He have despayur.

'Fool,' lissurd say.

'Soft,' say dandyline.

'Week,' say flutterby.

Bird see him. She know how hard is life without love.

'What take sad away?' she say.

'Red rose,' he say.

She sertch far more wide than he. But still she find only wite roses, yello roses.

Day over, she riturn to garden. She rest on bare brantchur of red rose tree.

'One rose is all he want,' she say to tree.

'Erth is too cold,' tree say.

'Let my fethers warm yoo,' she say.

'One rose?'

'Yes.'

'Very well. Sing all nite. As yoo sing, press agenst me till my thorns peerce. As blood flow, one rose grow, one rose fill with red.'

'How much blood?'

'All.'

'Much to give for one rose.'

Last lite of sun fall. Bird press agenst rose tree, sing. Of hope, payshunse, true harts. What lovers feel, what lovers give. Soft tutch. Warm lips. Sweet kiss.

Pettul by pettul, leef by leef, rose grow. Wite then pink then more dark red as bird sing more loud. Trees drop brantchurs to lissun more close. Moon shed silva tears. Sun rise erly to hear.

Rose open pettuls in cold morning air.

'All perfect,' say rose tree. 'All finish.'

Bird make no arnsa. Thorn in hart, she lie ded in tall grass. Cold wind blow through garden, shake brantchurs on every tree. Boy heer, look up from book. See perfect red rose.

'What luck,' he say.

He cry out with joy, cut it from tree, rush to where true love live.

Rap in warm blankits, she sit on soft cushins. Sweet strorberrys lay before on wood plate.

'Do I take one more?' she think.

Brite eyes spark. Long black hair shine like cleer nite sky. She look up as boy stand before her.

'Deer love, I bring yoo red rose,' he say.

She smile sweet smile. Drop chin. Rinkle nose. Point to table behind. Scatter with ten yello roses.

'Son of Brenin bring these,' she say. 'Also these.'

She point to strorberrys.

'Also this.'

She point to silva clip in hair.

'Also this.'

On dress is clip in shape of, color of red rose. She tutch it.

'This last forever,' she say. 'Soon yors die.'

He leeve, riturn to garden, throw rose on ground, stamp on it, see ded bird, kick it away.

'Love is for idjurts,' he say.

#

Since Howul leave Blanow, gold is become brown season. Now he have save him twice, he is only one Ista trust. It make him even more high up. Above Loyd.

He know what this mean. When you think all is good, this is when roofs collapse and rocks fall. From this time on he will make them fall, not be under them.

After daughters of Griff try to kill him, Ista stay alway in flower pictures room. He no more try to please anyone. If they want something they can gofuck. Howul and Loyd is only ones allow to see him. All he think about is that any moment someone will try to kill him again. He think people add something to water he drink or wash with. He only drink water Howul bring him. And he stink.

He sit now in tall wood chair and stare at pictures like he keep expect the flowers in them to move or say something. For keep him safe, Howul want something back. Too oft now he think of Blanow. Jen. Erin. Challenge. Gommel. Good things also. The smell of lemon thyme, cook potatos, jasmine. Nobody Beach. The sun as it rise above the grey cliffs. Place for Lookout.

'With six Padded Men and six guns,' he say, 'I can go to Blanow and make it Kimry again for you.'

Ista no more seem interest. It is many day since he last ask of Blanow. Howul do so much already for the rancid turd, this is least he can give back, isnt? The turd stare at anemones, say nothing. So Howul carry on.

'This way, you do what no Brenin do before. And make Blanow Kimry is best way to make you safe also.'

'How?'

'You show everyone what strong Brenin you is. And there is plants in Blanow you do not have here.'

'We do not need plants.'

'Depend what they do, isnt? These make you sleep, make you weak, make you accept.'

Ista tcha.

'We do not need any of that,' he say.

'Not you. Kings People. With plants you can make them so. All of them. Even Loyd.'

'Accept us?'

'Yes. And I tell you before of invisibilly flower. Eat it and they cannot see you.'

Ista think a while then say –

'You can get them for us from Blanow?'

'Yes.'

'Send someone else to get them. If you go, they kill us. Blanow already give us what we need. You must stay here and keep us safe.'

The turd say No to him again. He cannot get away because Blanow have already give Ista what he need. Blanow have give Ista Howul.

If Howul cannot go to Blanow with Padded Men, perhap he go to Nowhere instead. Then he is more close to Blanow.

It is crap plan but best he can think of.

'Here is what I do for you. I go to Nowhere. I take Loyd with me. In Nowhere I get Padded Men to 'finish finish' him for you. How is that?'

No answer. He sleep? He die? He see anemone petals move at last?

'You hear what I say?'

Still nothing. After too many day alone, Ista now hear and see only what is inside hims head. Howul tap side of Istas chair with hims foot and say –

'You hear me? Nowhere.'

Something drop or fall out of Istas mind and it unstick.

'I need you here to make potch for me,' he say.

'I learn someone else.'

'Also to save me. Protect me. Others all want to kill me. I need you.'

And now all get strange. Big strong Brenin who piss on everyone begin to cry.

Evil fuck have just say No to me again, think Howul. But he do not like that Ista cry. He want it to stop. So he say to him what he say to Erin when she cry, what Mags say to him when he cry.

'Easy now. All will be well. I make it all so. I promise.'

#

In home this night, as well as feet rub and toesys squeeze, Tegwin have fingers rub and shoulders squeeze, head rub and ears squeeze, knees rub and calfs squeeze. While this hap, Howul talk to her of how Kings People now creep to him, show off to him, want from him.

'You like that they creep to you?' she say.

'It mean I can help others who deserve. And get Ista to do as I wish.'

'You wish to go back to Blanow and kill those who kill your daughter. He help you do this?'

He think he is special and straightway she show him he is not.

'Not yet. You say before there is much I do not understand. Tell me how I get Ista to help me do this.'

'There is much I do not understand neither. I do not know how you do this.'

All this time and still he is no more close to go back. Do she not know? Or do she know and not say? He get so little from her. Alway so calm and wary. Now he try to change that.

'Here is what I can do. Tell him for real what hap to Morgan and others. Tell him all. He never like Morgan. It will please him and he will help me.'

As he say this, she send scanks away and sit up.

'You must not,' she say.

'Why not? He will do as I ask to thank me. I will go with Padded Men to Blanow.'

'If you tell him, next Loyd will know. If Loyd know what you do to hims brother, all is finish for you and me.'

'So help me with things I do not understand.'

Squeeze and rubs of feet, toesys, fingers, shoulders, head, ears, knees and calfs have give glow to her face that he cannot take eyes from. She is more keriss to him now than ever. Calm and wary, she let him wait. Spider in web or frost before thaw? He do not know.

'Tell me, Howul,' she say at last.

There is so much. He start with something he hope is simple.

'Caddick. Who replace him now? Who is now in Nowhere?'

'No one yet. Ista have not decide yet. Ista is bad at decide.'

He have plenty else to ask like this. Where is keep tinfoods in Kimry. How many villages is outside. Why everyone hate Ista. Easy. Simple. But he cannot help himself. So glow, so keriss. He ask this instead.

'You say before we just help each other. Nothing more. Why nothing more?'

'You want to know why I will not be your woman?'

Again she cut through and beyond, like she know what he mean before he do.

'Yes. And how I can change it.'

'So I will be your woman?'

'Yes.'

'You is good man but I will not be your woman.'

'Never?'

'Never.'

As with Milani and Beth, Tegwin is woman he want more the more he cannot have. For this he know he is idiot. He is defeat. He must accept. He will accept.

Is she please that he ask? Angry? He have not the foggyrest. With Jen all is so much more easy. He know what she think because she tell him. If she is not please, she say. If she want something, she say.

'Things in Blanow is different,' he say.

'So you keep tell me.'

She smile to show she is not mean nor hard.

'How do I know what you want?'

'How do you know what I want?'

She say it back like every word is new to her.

'Yes.'

Long Tegwin wait. Then –

'Yes, things is different in Blanow. You want to know what I want? You ask, isnit? You never ask. You just say what you want. It is not the same.'

Howul is amaze by how much idiot he is.

'Sorry,' he say.

Last time he say this to her is after he near kill her. He think she now remember it, same as him. He want to ask but do not. What she want, not what he want.

'What you want now?' he ask.

'Toesys squeeze, feet rub and sleep.'

Accept. Accept. As he go to door, she call after him.

'Ista stay strong by make others fight,' she say. 'He make high ups fear and hate each other. No one is safe.'

She mean him? Or her? Or both?

For Howul, all Kimry is complicate.

#

More he think about Blanow again, more something keep scratch and bite and jab at him. Tegwin have say all scanks is Kings People who is punish but there is too many for that. Where is others from? Ista have say one time –

'Blanow already give us what we need.'

Howul have suppose he mean him, Madbad who keep Ista safe. Now he is not sure.

He remember the skinbone snotnoses he have see outside in the pit as he first arrive in Kimry. With them is a baby with deep purple bruise on neck and back.

He go now out of the huge grey building and over the deep water trench to the higgurdy path that run by the pits. He get to the pit with the snotnoses. The Padded Men there pull back some corrygate iron fence and let him through. He is Kings People and Istas favourite. Of course they let him through.

A steep path lead down to dry hard earth at the bottom. A wood hut stand here, its door a long dusty piece of thick red cloth. He pull it back and step through.

Bad air from outside mix with dust and bad air inside. Smoke, sweat, farts, decay. The room is split in half by more dusty red cloth. In front half on a wood floor sit the same naked snotnoses as before. The growup skinbone who before have baby to breast now lie on the floor and sleep. The baby is next to her and a season more big than before. All is quiet and still.

The growup hear Howul and stand up with look of fright pigeon. Because she stand up the snotnoses stand up also. The baby look at Howul and start to cry. The growup try to shush him.

'He is your baby?' Howul ask.

Her face go blank and she say nothing. As all scanks.

The bad thinking which bring Howul here now press more hard on him. The purple on babys back and neck is not a bruise. It is a birth stain. Murf, son of Glend and Jerry, have the same.

When Jims and Droo have take Murf to Field of Black, no gentle earth ever cover him. They have send him away instead. Here he is now. Little skinbone.

There is twenty other snotnoses. Jims and Droo have take

about as many to Field of Black in past eleven year. And many more before.

Howul remember some of them. Linds baby. Neeshas twins. Hims own son Idris after he and Jen have Erin. Hims two brothers. Many, many more. No earth, no gentle blanket, no peace, no safe now. Instead, they say nothing, serve Kings People, work in pits, go skinbone, go scank.

He take Murf and hold him in hims arms and sway and shush him.

The cloth draw back and two women come through from other side of hut. The yellow hair and black hair daughters of Griff. Hattie and Jessie. Except both now have shave heads and wear red rags.

'Why you here?' say Hattie.

He point to the skinbone snotnoses.

'These is Blanow, isnit?'

'Gofuck,' say Jessie.

Her sister lean back her head and fold her arms.

'Soon our father is Brenin again,' she say.

Baby Murf hiccup and throw a little vom onto Howuls arm. Growup skinbone step forward to take him.

'He is from Blanow?'

No answer from anyone.

'You is here because you attack Ista?'

The sisters do not say. He have bring rocksack with him. In it is tinfoods for everyone and a knife. He open them and hand them out. The daughters eat mush with thems fingers. When Howul give tinfoods to the skinbones, they look back in amaze. No one give them tinfoods before. He get them to copy how daughters eat.

'I can help you,' Howul say.

'How?' say Hattie.

'Tell me true. These is Blanow skinbones, isnit?'

Nothing. Howul take out four more tinfoods. He hold knife by them, ready to open.

'Tell me what you know.'

'Gofuck,' say Hattie.

He start to put the tinfoods away then catch the stare of every big eye snotnose. He open them and hand them out.

'You like it here? You want to stay?' say Howul.

'You is all Ista,' say Hattie.

'Gofuck,' say Jessie.

'Gofuck,' say Hattie.

This go well, think Howul. All hate me, as per the usual. He is not all Ista. Ista is the turd who say No to him, the Brenin who allow Murf and other Blanow babys to be treat this way.

He take out all the tinfoods still in hims rocksack and put them on the ground. He offer knife to Hattie. It is too small to hurt anyone much but will open tinfoods and may kill rats. She take it from him. He look again at the quiet, big eye snotnoses.

'You love your father, isnit?' he say to Hattie. 'I wish my daughter have love me as much.'

Baby Murf sleep now in hims arms. Howul kiss hims head.

'I is not all Ista,' he say. 'You help me, I help you and your father. Ista can gofuck.'

As he carry Murf out of the hut, Hattie say –

'Baby is Blanow.'

He carry Murf back along higgurdy path. When they get to the huge grey building, he put hims finger in Murfs mouth so he wont cry and hide him with sleeve of robe.

He go straight to Catrins room. Since her baby and man die, he go see her so she can talk more of them. The room is clean and smell no more of disease. No mess. No bloat body.

'You can look after him?' he ask.

Catrin get up from a chair and take Murf from him.

So far the rocks he make fall all land where he want them to.

He have work out how Blanow babys get here. Of course. Rids house in Tangrish. The tall grass outside it. The dark cellar that smell of stale water, earth and soot. The narrow tunnel, plastycrates, the big wood box on wheels, the huge metal door. The door that join Blanow to Tangrish and People Outside. Blanow give Kimry baby Murf, Howuls baby brothers, baby son and many others. And what do Kimry give Blanow? Tinfoods, bottles, barley dust.

Anger rage in Howul. He want to get metal stick from a Padded Man, go to the soft room with the thick carpet and fancy pictures and smash out Istas brains. But he know this help no one. All this with babys have hap longtime. All Kimry and Blanow Brenins must know. Featherwoman must know. And Caddick. Rid. Who else?

He go to Room of State, then up steps and through long room with two lines of candles. There is no Padded Men anywhere. He pull back the cloth door and enter flower pictures room.

Loyd sit in Istas chair. Howul have only see Ista in it before. And Loyd do not just sit. He also point a gun at Ista.

'Save us,' say Ista.

'Go away,' say Loyd.

Of a sudden there is noise outside. First through the door is daughters of Griff, Hattie and Jessie. Behind them is old man with bright red burns all over hims face. Griff. All is now dress as Kings People. With them is Tegwin.

The daughters each have big knife. Ista step away from them till wall with anemones picture stop him. He stand still as Griff move forward, also with knife. He close hims eyes then scream as Griff stab. He slump to the floor and bleed. The daughters hug each other.

Ista open hims eyes again and stare up at Howul.

'You promise us,' he say.

Griff is old but strong from time he spend bash at hot metal in pit. He get down on haunches and lift Ista up so they is eye to eye. Blood wash over Griffs hands as he speak.

'We is send to pit because of lies you tell,' he say. 'Now everyone see what a shooky, cunty shitebag you is. It all work well for you, isnit?'

Istas eyes no more have light in them. Griff drop him and stand up. Loyd stand up also.

'Sweet revenge is best serve cold,' he say. 'He get what he deserve.'

Everyone except Howul and Tegwin seem excite by what hap.

Griff walk over to Howul.

'You is Istas favourite, isnit,' he say.

He have knife in hims hand. Istas blood still drip from it.

'Many here want you dead. Many hate you. You save Ista. You help Ista.'

'I save all who is sick.'

'You send our daughters to the pits.'

'Ista send them after I save him.'

'Loyd say we cannot trust you.'

Floor is sticky with Istas blood. Everyone seem to close in on Howul though no one move.

'Loyd is wrong,' he say. 'I try to help your daughters. I bring them tinfoods.'

Griff tcha. Hattie and Jessie say nothing. Tegwin go over to Griff. She rest hand on hims shoulder, lean in and gentle kiss hims cheek.

'You can trust him,' she say.

He put hims arm through hers and pull her more close to him. He is her man and now she have him back.

Next is like part in story where bad Brenin say with thumb if Gladilator live or die. All in room look from Howul to Griff then Griff to Howul then Howul to Griff again. At last Griff speak.

'They say you want to go to Blanow and make it Kimry. Correct?'

Howul nod.

'You can do this?'

'With six Padded Men and six guns. Yes.'

'Very well. It shall be arrange. But fail and yours is red rags and hot pit. Get?'

Howul get.

#

JOURNEY

After so much time of wait, now of a sudden all rocks fall in place. All rocks? Most rocks. He have ask for six Padded Men with six guns. He get three Padded Men with three guns and three metal sticks.

When he return to Blanow, will he make it all Kimry? Of course no. He make it all Howul. Now he know where scanks is from, Kimry deserve nothing. Instead, he make himself new Blanow Brenin. He punish Mister Yorath, Tall Nole, Jims and Droo for what they do to Erin. Milani is hims woman. And no more Blanow babys is give for tinfoods.

This, he now understand, is why he is save, why nothing ever kill him, why he is the one lemon thyme seed from hundreds not eat by insects nor blow into the sea nor rot but survive and grow. He is special. He is choose. He can now make bad things good.

All in Blanow will love him. All will give thanks.

Howul ask to speak to Tegwin one last time before he leave. Again they is in her home but now she is too busy for scank rubs and squeezes.

'I do not have long,' she say.

He have know nothing of plan to kill Ista. He do not regret it hap. But he do not understand why she have save him.

'Why have you save me?' he ask.

'Because of what I say before. You is good man.'

'You is with Griff when he is Brenin before?'

'Of course.'

'So why you not tell me this?'

She welcome this like fish welcome air but for once give answer.

'Less people know, less they can hurt you,' she say.

'I try to help you, not hurt you,' he say.

'One time you near kill me.'

This silence him.

'If there is more you want to ask me, you can ask me when you return,' she say.

'You want me to go now?'

'Yes.'

'I go. But one last thing.'

'No. That is it.'

'Thank you is all. That is last thing. Thank you.'

She smile. Perhap because she is please. Perhap because she know for sure he leave now.

He go to where the three Padded Men wait for him. They is Arron, Effan and Nino. Brothers. With them is no donkeys. Instead, the thin leg, sharp spike creatures he first see among the bare earth and white rocks near Tangrish. Goats. Six of them with leatherbags on thems backs. The brothers pull them along with rope. They carry much less than donkeys but also stop less, eat less and make less noise. And make good meat. Before too many day, six is five.

In one leatherbag is the books scanks get for Howul. No matter they is heavy and fill with gobbledybollocks. Now he is special, one day they will all make sense to him.

Howul also bring Ivor with him. Ivor is the young skinbone from the room where Loyd and Howul heal Kings People. Who hand over tablets and potch and look more ill than those they is for. One day, Howul will make all skinbones Kings People and stop Kimry take babys from Blanow. For now, he can just treat Ivor more well.

Hims plan is this. Go to Nowhere. Hope to go on to Tangrish. Hope to go on to Blanow. Another perfect Howul plan.

The brothers take them on the same wide, flat path Howul and Tegwin walk on to get to Kimry. It go through same villages with same Brenins, naked snotnoses and half starve growups as before. As they travel, the brothers talk plenty to each other and little to Howul. Every day they fall out, make up, gang up, sulk, love, hate. Any at any time can do any of this and any other can at any time side with or oppose. Arron like to show he is best by carry most or walk most fast or drink most or eat most or cough most loud or spit most. Effan show it by think most or talk most or listen most or scratch chin most or look at brothers like they is idiots most. Nino show it by smile most and praise most. Bullyboy, brains and bumsuck.

Most Padded Men spend all thems time in stand around, guard, look fierce, do not move. Every day they get bored enough to chew fist off while more and more nothing hap. Kings People say little to them. Not Howul. He talk to Arron,

Effan and Nino of Blanow. He tell them who is most strong there, who must be put on trial, who they can and cannot trust, which buildings and places they must make safe for him. As he do this, they look at feet and say nothing. Before, Padded Men torture him when he do not speak of Blanow. Now they cannot wait for him to stop.

Even though he never say anything back, Howul prefer to talk to Ivor than Padded Men. Most scanks show nothing but blank faces to Kings People. Young Ivor show more than this and find way to answer Howul without speak. With shake or nod head, hold up fingers for numbers etcetera etcetera. Yes, he is bring to Kimry from Blanow. Yes, the pit for skinbone snotnoses is hims first Kimry home. Yes, there is no old scanks in Kimry. Yes, the work is too hard for long life.

This is another reason Howul like to talk to Ivor. He know hims brothers by now must have die in Kimry. They is too old still to live. But not hims son. Name Idris, he and Jen have lose him to Field of Black twelve year back. He is take from them when he have just seven month. Same as Jen and Erin, he have brown eyes, frizzy black mess hair, dark skin, top lip that rest on bottom lip like it hide a hazelnut under it. Big nose like Howul. Ivor have all these things also. Way he care for sick Kings People is how Howul one time care for people in Blanow.

More time Howul spend with Ivor, more he believe it is true. Idris is Ivor. Ivor is Idris. Ivor is hims son.

He say nothing of this to him yet. Wait till he do something for him to make hims life more good. Else second time in hims sons life he is just crap father to him.

If ever Ivor wish Howul say and share less, he never show it. He make it seem he want alway to hear more. He listen, smile, nod, speak with hands. A good son.

Village Brenins is village Brenins. When they see he is Kings People, they say nothing and bring tinfoods, vegetables, fruit, water, beer. Beds to lie on. As Howul leave, alway he give them circles of metal.

From last village they take path that pass near where Howul have kill Morgan and Padded Men. He remember the scrape metal smell from so much blood, the dust and mud they roll in. Every hit, every scream, every try they make to get up again.

Howul can see the pond, circle of rocks and brambles where all have hap. He think he can see bones also.

'We need water,' say Arron and move toward pond.

'There is water in Nowhere,' say Effan and stay on path. 'Nowhere is close.'

Nino look at both and, weary of foot, decide he prefer less walk. He stay on path with Effan. Arron tcha and return to them. Howuls secret stay secret.

Soon they is at Nowhere. Wind have blow down part of wall and one wood building. The well still give them water but there is no tinfoods here now, no plastycrates, knifes, spoons, bows, arrows, plates, candles. Shelfs, floors, rooms is empty.

'Villages take it,' say Effan.

'When we return, each will get some,' say Arron.

He do not mean tinfoods.

No donkeys is here now neither. Perhap they lie in dust all day with nothing on thems backs and lush grass only a roll over away. More like they have fill the stomachs of village Brenins.

'You is here before?' say Howul.

'Yes,' say Effan. 'Alway it is us or Bron, Gary and Phil.'

Bron is No Ear, Gary is Big Lips and Phil is Squishface Ugly Fuck.

'All good men, isnit?' say Nino.

'You is here when they die?' say Effan.

'They die before I get here. And Morgan. Only Tegwin still live. I heal her. But she say also they is all good men.'

With no tinfoods on shelfs for them, they eat goat instead. Six that is already become five now become four. They sit, drink water, eat. All except Ivor. He stand. And never drink nor eat in front of others and only when others is finish. This I will change, think Howul.

The villages have take beds also so they lie on floor to sleep. When they wake, Arron want to go back to most near village and kick heads. Effan want to move on. Again Nino want what mean less walk.

Howul is Kings People but alway let them decide where to go next. After all, only they know where each place is.

Thems next journey is same as Howul make before with Caddick after Steve leave them. After five day, they reach place of earth, scrub and rocks. Here brothers make big fire then throw on it wet leafs, branches and grass to make high smoke. This is how they tell Tangrish they is here.

Even Padded Men do not know way through deep and shallow water that lead to Tangrish. Steve arrive next day. He grab and hug each like they is son or brother.

'My heart is open for you. All is Okay?'

Howul tell him all is Okay.

#

TANGRISH

Back in place of plenty and home for Gold People, Steve take them first to Featherwoman.

'We welcome you all with open heart,' she say.

And with potatos, onions, spinach and cool, clean water. Like village Brenins, Gold People know who they must be good to.

Beth and Emlin join them. Beths hands is on her swellup stomach.

'Pregnens, isnit?' she say.

'Soon she will have baby, isnit?' say Emlin.

'We is glad you is back,' say Beth. 'It make good day even more good. Already today Shiel have see a chiffchaff and a chaffinch and Owin find a mulberry tree.'

'You have hungry?' ask Steve.

Howul shove spinach and potato in hims mouth as they speak so he do not need say anything back. Thems shiny good cheer already annoy him. Since he last see them he have kill four men. Soon, more. He do no want to hear of chiffchaff and mulberry trees.

After they finish eat, Gold People take them into The Shapple. Everyone stand as Featherwoman close her dead eyes and hold up her hands.

'Let us give thanks for the good things we have,' she say. 'For the food we eat and the water we drink, for the clothes we wear and the sun that shine on us. For the happy, healthy baby Beth will soon have. And let us give thanks also for the safe return of Howul and greet with warm open heart all those he have bring to us.'

Featherwoman lift one leg high then stamp it on ground then do same with other. Gold People close eyes and make footstamps. Howul do same. Ivor copy him. The brothers stand still with arms fold and watch. Howul is sorry when it stop. No matter it look weird. It feel good.

As everyone leave The Shapple, Beth groan and hold her stomach. Other Tangrish women come over to her.

Not much blood. Not many screams. No collapse. No death. A happy, healthy, plumpy boy in time it take to heat water. Gold People have gold babys too.

Rid is not at The Shapple so Howul go to hims home to find him. Stink of ganja hit him as he go in. Stink of Rid also. Round hims feet is empty tinfoods and hootch bottles. Flies swarm them.

Rid lie back in a soft chair and sleep. Howul tap hims shoulder to wake him. Then tap and tap again. Then hit hard.

Rid look round and stand up. A empty tinfood fall on the floor. He watch as it roll toward Howul and stop less than two fingers from him. He stare amaze as if just by look at it Howul have make it stop.

'Hiya Rid,' say Howul.

Hims teeny eyes is sore and red. They look but do not see. He do not know who Howul is. He do not know who he is.

'When they so he do,' he say, 'till they under it and then because I have say when but it is against so they do not if there is, isnit? Till they have take with where because in the fields. If it do not. He have say me and I have say and then he have when there is because of them.'

He cough, spit on the floor and go back to sleep.

Rid have do as Howul have ask. No more mushrooms. Trouble is, he find Tangrish fuckbuggery dull. So he have switch to just ganja instead. And hootch.

Howul return with Ivor and for three day they stay with him and keep him away from anything he might smoke, eat or drink. While Rid sleep, sweat, shake and shiver, they clear up hims mess till the stink is more easy to bear and there is room for them to sit on floor. Ivor do as ask, never complain, still never speak.

'One day soon,' Howul say to him, 'your life will be much more than it is now. One day soon I will be Blanow Brenin.'

A red-eye fly stay a moment too long on the floor in front of him. He strike at it and miss. No matter. Soon all will be good. The punish he will give to some. The food and blankets he will give to others. He will change things for everyone. Less fear. Less lies. No tinfoods. More potch. More storys. More straight. More true. And a good, good life for hims son.

He do not yet know how all this will hap. But who else have do what he have? Places he go, things he do, deaths he scape. Compare with all that, what is next is easy.

The fly is back. This time Ivor strike. He do not miss. He pick up what remain, open door and flick it away. Rid groan, turn over, sleep on.

Now, think Howul. Now.

'There is something I want you to know, Ivor.'

He tell him what he have want to tell longtime. All the reasons why Ivor is Idris and Idris Ivor. Same age. Same big nose. Same eyes and hair as mum and sis. Can run fast, see good. Can learn quick. Clever.

'You is my son for sure,' he say.

Howul want to hug him, promise alway to be good father. Too early. Too weird. So he say instead there is less flys now and stink is not so bad.

Ivor of course say nothing. He seem please but perhaps he just want to please Howul.

Rid groan again and wake up. Hims head still hurt too much for him to open hims eyes but at least he can hear.

'Blanow need your help,' say Howul. 'All need you. All will thank you.'

'I cannot,' say Rid.

Rid is Blanow and Tangrish and Kimry, only person who connect all. Bad choice for Howul. Only choice for Howul. And simple in what he need.

'Here. Have this.'

Howul hand him ganja and spark stick.

Rid hold hims hurt head as he sit up and try to to answer what Howul ask. When and how huge metal door between Tangrish and Blanow is open and who open it. At start of every season at first light, Rid say, Jims bang on door one time. If Rid then bang on door three time, this tell Blanow that many tinfoods from Kimry is ready to bring in. Both return in middle of day for swap.

When is start of white season? Next day. No long wait for Howul. He is special. He is choose. Rocks fall where he want. There is no new tinfoods from Kimry for Blanow but Jims will not know this. When he bang on door one time, still Rid will bang on door three time. Jims will open. And Howul will return.

When footstamps finish this night, Howul tell Featherwoman he have questions for her. Because he is now Kings People, she let him ask. But first she take him to her home. It is no more big than those other Gold People have with same wood furniture, soft bed, plumpy cushions etcetera

etcetera. Gold People already have so much even Brenin do not need more.

With no sight, Featherwoman still know where all is and find everything she reach for easy. Two wood chairs is push in on same side of table. She pull them out and move them so they now face each other with only small space between. This is where they sit. She pick up pattycake from table, brack and offer part of it to Howul.

'I have no hungry,' he say.

'It is ceremony,' she say.

He take it, bite some and swallow. It is dry so he drop rest on floor.

'All finish,' he say.

'You drop some,' she say. 'It is too dry to finish all.'

Next she pick up bottle from table, pour red liquid from it into glass without spill and offer.

'Drink,' she say.

It taste like most sour cherrys. He want to pour rest away but think she will know if he do this. So he swallow it then say —

'Finish.'

'It is good we talk,' she say. 'I is sad you leave and glad for your return. Why you here? Is you new Caddick?'

He have see how much they do for Caddick. Will all be more easy if he say Yes? Most like. But she know straightway of hims pattycake billybully even without see. He decide to say what is true.

'I is not here for items. I is here to get to Blanow. I need your help.'

'Why get to Blanow?'

'It is my home.'

'You take the men with guns with you?'

'Yes.'

'Why?'

'Blanow kill my daughter. There must be trial.'

She tcha. He never hear her tcha before.

'Some time it make sense to accept.'

'Yes. But this is not that time.'

'You cannot get to Blanow.'

'I find way here. I find way back.'

Again she tcha and now stand so he have to look up at her.

When he go to stand she push him back down again. She is strong as Padded Men.

'All is fill with peace here,' she say. 'Alway we is good to you, Howul. We heal you and look after you. I ask you not to do this.'

'I do this for my daughter.'

'We all lose people.'

'I do not lose her. She is kill.'

Again he try to stand. Again she push him down.

'You think I is still some shiteforbrain Madbad?'

'I never think this.'

'I have guns now.'

'You let sad stop you from do what make sense. I learn this, Howul. Kill do not mend. Kill alway make more bad.'

'You do not know bad. Only bad thing in Tangrish is if it rain or someones spade is brack.'

'I do not argue bad with you.'

Of course. Her no sight is also bad. She do so well without it is easy to forget. He remember now and use. Instead of try to stand, he throw himself down to right side. Then roll away and stand before she can reach or stop him. As they speak, he keep back away from her. Between words, he move alway to a new place. It make her more weak.

'Why you let them?' he say.

'Let who?'

'My son. My brothers. Baby Murf. You let them through, isnit? Why?'

Now she sit. She offer more red liquid. He say No. She do not offer again.

'For true, we let them through. But it is not what I wish. It is what must be.'

Same old gobbledybollocks.

'If you wish, you can stop it.'

'Then what? Blanow take from us what belong to us? Kimry same? This way, all stay safe. It is best.'

'Not for Idris. Not for Murf. Not for my brothers.'

'If they stay in Blanow, what then? There is not enough food in Blanow. You know this. Before you have think they is all kill, isnit. This way is more good for them. This way everyone can live.'

Another shooky Brenin, same as rest.

'You cannot stop me. I is choose.'
'You have change, Howul.'
'Yes. And so must all else.'
He do a few footstamps just for her as he leave.

#

Before first light, Howul and Padded Men and Ivor is at Rids home to wake him. It only take shouts, face slaps and pour water and soon he know who they is and why they is here. Rid have steal so many tinfoods before that still he have plenty in hims home. And empty plastycrates. Howul get brothers to put some tinfoods in the crates but Rid try to stop them.

'They is mine,' he say. 'They is all I have till Caddick return.'

'He is back soon,' say Howul.

A huge lie that do not seem to bother Padded Men. For them, think Howul, this is just how Kings People is.

'We is friends now, isnit, Rid?'

Rid scowl and nod.

'What I do for you now is best any friend ever can do for any other.'

'Steal my tinfoods?'

'Where we go, you do not need them.'

'What you mean?'

'Why you think I go to Blanow?'

'You want to go home, isnit.'

'Correct. And you know what I do when I get there?'

'Dob?'

'You want to be Blanow Brenin, isnit?'

'Yes. I is promise.'

'I want this for you also. I go there to make you Blanow Brenin. You have wait too long already. This is what I do for you as friend.'

Howul have tell Padded Men he is new Blanow Brenin. Now he tell Rid different. Again they say nothing.

'When I is Blanow Brenin,' say Rid, 'still I need your help. I think.'

'I will free give it.'

'Any home you want in Blanow is yours, except Big

House. All else also. Tinfoods –'

Rid stop, think.

'Mister Yorath is Brenin. I must wait till he die, isnit,' he say.

'Some time Brenin must do what is brave. Who is more good Brenin – you or him?'

'Me?'

'Yes, of course. That is why I make you Brenin. Blanow need you. You think Mister Yorath is same good friend as I is?'

'He say I will be Brenin.'

'He do not mean it. He say it so he can leave you here. You like it here?'

'No.'

'No good friend do this to you. He know you is more good Brenin than he is so he send you away. Also, you remember Milani?'

'Yes.'

'You like how she look?'

'Of course. She is most keriss in Blanow.'

'After you leave she tell me how much she have want you.'

'Milani? She never show this.'

'Mister Yorath take her so you cannot have her.'

'She call me scrunty shiteface.'

'He tell her to say this. But Milani say different. She tell me she want you to dob her.'

'Me?'

'Yes. And Big Tris. She say same thing.'

Howul begin to feel bad how easy he find it to billy bully Rid. But he do not stop.

'Help us and all you ever want is yours.'

'For real?'

'For real. Just help us get into Blanow. I take it and come back for you. Promise.'

They lower the plastycrates into the cellar near Rids house, put them in the big wood box then move this along the straight metal lines till they reach the huge metal door. Howul and Ivor hide in one crate, the brothers in the others. Howul then get Rid to put tinfoods on top to hide them.

It is trick he learn from Geeks and Ojays story. They fight so long they forget why. When Geeks can fight no more, they tell Ojays they win. Next day, they is disappear and leave gifts for Ojays – wood crates fill with tinfoods, hootch, candles. Ojays put weapons away, eat, drink, sleep. Safe at last. Except Geeks never go. They hide instead under tinfoods. They climb out now and turn Ojays blood into rivers. Beware Geeks.

Howul hear bang on metal door then three more then open. Someone greet Rid. Droo. Why Droo? Where is Jims?

A baby sniff and snort and begin to cry.

'This one is a good boy some time,' say Droo and try to shush him.

He fail.

'He want tittie,' say Droo. 'They both want tittie.'

Two babys.

'Get some soon,' say Rid.

Tinfoods is swap for them. If Howul climb out now he can save babys. But then he cannot be sure to reach Blanow. He do not yet know what is beyond metal door.

He wait as Droo tell Rid what hap in Blanow since they last see him. Who is well, who work hard, who complain. Rid say little back but still it go on longtime. Droo explain how Harol have make Jims angry by brack the water pump then Jims get Tall Nole to kick Harols arse. Both laugh.

'How is Milani?' say Rid.

'Milani? Why?' say Droo.

'Have she speak of me?'

'No. Most in Blanow forget you, isnit?'

'Tell her I is well.'

The first baby have set other off and both now cry loud.

'Till next time,' say Droo.

He push the wood box through door and lock it behind him. Rid keep babys. Beth soon have extra mouths to feed.

Soon I make this stop, think Howul.

#

BLANOW

Wood box is stop by another metal door. Droo bang on it four time and hear same back. Door is open and he push box through. They is in same tunnel but now on Blanow side.

'Let us push together,' say Droo.

'Okay,' say another voice.

Tall Noles. Still no Jims.

They have not push far when the box speak to them.

'Now,' it say.

Tall Nole and Droo step back in amaze as Howul and the others climb out.

'Fuck in a bucket,' say Tall Nole.

'Droo. Tall Nole,' say Howul.

'Where is the other tinfoods?' say Tall Nole.

'There is us instead,' say Howul.

'What you want?' say Droo.

'Mister Yorath,' say Howul.

'We cannot,' say Droo.

The brothers point guns at him. He seem to know what guns is.

'Follow me,' he say.

They leave wood box where it is and walk on along the tunnel to another cellar of the People Before. Brick walls, slope floor, stale air, damp. Stone steps lead up from it to where a square piece of wood close them in. Droo pull at two handles and open it. They climb out.

Round them now is a thick green wall make from leeland trees. Howul have see it many time from The Green. It hide Field of Black.

The air is white season cold. Sun catch the tree tops and turn some of the green bright yellow. Though far back from the sea, all can straightway taste salt. There is no field in Field of Black. Instead is mud and open pits fill with bones. People bones. Blanow bones. No gentle earth cover them.

This I will change also, think Howul.

Droo take them to a small gap in the leelands. He pull back branches so they can go through. Soon they is on the path that lead past Big House and The Senter to The Green. The sky is Blanow, not Kimry. It carry no thick grey smoke. The smell is of lemon thyme and rosemary.

Howul have return. Strong, fierce, ready to make more rocks fall.

As they approach The Green, more and more people come to look at them. Three big men in thick padded clothes. A boy teen in red rags. A man in a blue robe they have never expect to see again. They say nothing and stare.

'Get Mister Yorath,' say Howul in loud new Brenin voice.

Droo and Tall Nole move toward Big House but Effan stop them.

'I go with,' he say. 'I make sure there is no arsy farsy.'

'Good,' say Howul.

He and others walk over to the fire by The Green. Big Tris cook pattycakes on the hot metal that sit on it. In her hand is a pattycake she have pick up to taste but this is not why her mouth open so big. She have see a dead man walk.

'You have two for me, isnit?' say Howul.

Of a sudden she feel the heat from the pattycake she hold. She drop it on the ground and close her mouth. Then open it again as she tip two pattycakes onto a wood plate and give them to Howul.

'And for my friends,' he say.

Big Tris give out two pattycakes also to Arron and Nino. Ivor stay back so Howul offer him one from hims own plate.

'If you have hungry,' say Howul.

Ivor take it but do not eat.

'You can eat also,' say Howul.

It is like he ask Ivor to jump in fire pit. Never have he see anyone with pattycake look more worry.

'Or more late on,' he say.

Ivor smile and hold pattycake and do not eat.

Arron and Nino take more pattycakes. They eat so many there is now only a few still on the hot metal for everyone else. Howul look at those who have gather.

'Who have hungry?' he ask them.

Slow but sure everyone raise thems arms. Big Tris also.

'I will change that for you,' he say.

It is a big promise from someone who have just give all thems pattycakes away.

'Why you here?' someone shout.

She move forward so he can see more good who it is.

Glend, mother of Murf. She throw both arms in the air to show how not please she is to see him.

'Everyone is glad when you leave,' she say. 'You come back to make everything bad again? Who is they?'

She point at Arron and Nino.

'Friends,' say Howul.

Perhaps the miss she still have for baby Murf and her man Jerry push away fear and let her speak more free. More like she just think Howul is still Howul from before. Half starve nobody grumpscrut who bring trouble alway. She do not want him back. He look round at others. Si, Robut, Ken, Treva, Fred, Milani, Andi, Gale, Nic, Eddy, Rona, Pat, Kim, Crayg, Reeta. So many he have heal and help. Hims daughter kill, him also if he have not scape. Do no one care? No. No one else want him back neither.

Of course, he think. This is how Blanow is. When all is bad, when all starve and struggle, there is no rise up against those who make this hap. Instead there is accept and complain. Then blame someone or something else that you cannot change. If Howul have not defy the Brenin and leave, everything now is more good. Howul spoil it for them.

Idiots, he think. Still, I can easy show them how they is wrong. I can put on same creep smile other Brenins use and promise to stop all bad things. I can tell what hap with Murf and other babys and how I will stop this.

'There is something you do not know about what go on here,' he say.

Glend shout at him again.

'Do not speak, Howul,' she say. 'We do not listen. Go away and stop make trouble.'

Someone now walk toward them from Big House with Droo, Tall Nole and Effan. Not Mister Yorath. Mister Jims. Slow ceremony walk, chin high, arms fold over. He wear white shirt, black coat, black britches and black hat of People Before. Same as Mister Yorath have wear.

Tall Nole place the laddyback chair down for Mister Jims. Slow ceremony sit. Mister Jims look straight ahead like nothing matter except him. Blanow people is not surprise to see him. He is new Brenin to Howul but not to them.

He is not bother by Padded Men nor guns neither. Or perhaps he hide how scarify he is with ceremony and straight stare.

'Why you here, Howul?' he say.

'Where is Mister Yorath?' say Howul.

'When bad people do bad things, alway we make them pay.'

'You kill him?'

'No. He have leave us. And will not return. Why you here?'

'It is time for change.'

'Alway it is time for change.'

Mister Jims throw out a smile that everyone catch and is warm by. Best creep smile Howul ever see.

'Things is bad before. I make them good again,' he say. 'These is not stupid people. They know things is bad before. They know I make them good again.'

He say it twice to help the not stupid people full understand it. They smile back at him. They know it is not true but for a moment he make them believe it.

'Everyone know it,' say Mister Jims.

'You ask why I is here,' say Howul. 'I is here to be new Brenin.'

He walk onto small grass mound only for Brenin and nod at brothers to join him.

'It is time,' he say.

They seem in no hurry. They keep thems guns over thems backs and carry on eat pattycakes.

Tall Nole push Howul back off the mound.

'We have agree,' Howul say to the brothers. 'It is what Griff wish.'

As he go over to them, they take guns off thems backs and point them at him.

Mister Jims now stand.

'Of usual we do not welcome People Outside,' he say. 'But these is different. They bring Howul back to us. We must thank them, isnit.'

A few mutter thems thanks but most is still confuse and wary. Jims smile and point Effan out to them.

'This good man tell me all just now,' he say. 'He tell me Howul have run to thems village after he leave us. He arrive all fright and pissypants.'

Thanks is now laughs.

'He beg them to look after him. They is kind people so they

do this. But then he start to big gob about how he scape us after he do bad things here. He big gob so much they get sick of him.'

More laughs.

'They find way to bring him back and here he is.'

'Baby Murf live,' Howul shout at Glend. 'I know where he is.'

'More big gob,' say Jims.

Tall Nole and brothers approach him. Griff have not send Howul back to take Blanow. He have send him back so they can punish him. Effan and brothers have know this and just do as Griff ask. And Tegwin? Have she know also?

Cyclone blow, roof collapse, rocks bury. Everything is brack again. Howul is nobody grumpscrut.

#

They is in the room in Big House with the fridge again. Mister Jims sit where Mister Yorath sit before. The brothers and Tall Nole and Droo sit, drink hootch, drink beers, eat tinfoods. Howul stand. Ivor stand. Neither have hootch nor tinfoods.

Last time Howul is in this room, things do not go well for him. He expect no more now.

All others except Ivor is chuffy with smug and excite. Mister Jims tell the brothers how please he is with them, how they must thank thems Brenin for return slime to Blanow. By slime he mean Howul.

'What you do with him? Kill him?' say Arron who also mean Howul.

'That depend on him,' say Mister Jims. 'You is finish here now, isnit?'

'We can stay more long, if you want.'

'No need. Droo and Tall Nole show you way back.'

Jims want to be rid so he can ask Howul of Kimry and Tangrish. Then kill.

As he speak, Ivor bring more beers and tinfoods and put them on table in front of brothers. Effan stand up to leave but Arron and Nino stay sit and reach for beers. Jims give them creep smile.

'You is special guests,' he say. 'Take your time. Enjoy.'

Everything Howul wish for is dust now. Everything he try

to make hap have end bad. He can give Jims more billy bully. But what for? Nothing he say change anything. He cannot be Blanow Brenin. Someone will kill him now or soon. Why wait? He cannot give Ivor life he want to give. They will take hims son back to Kimry. Or kill him. Bad father to daughter. Bad father to son.

The creatures, diseases, weather, people he have fight before, alway it matter to him to win. Not now. He have fail in everything and everyone want him dead. Now even he want him dead.

'I is ready,' he say to Jims. 'Kill me now.'

This Jims have not expect.

'You will be punish,' he say. 'But first we talk.'

'I have nothing for you.'

'Still we talk.'

Tall Nole have finish hims tinfoods and drink.

'Get me more,' he say to Ivor.

Ivor go to fridge and bring Tall Nole and Droo tinfoods different to those before. They have paper round with picture of man who wear green leaf clothes. Next to him is pile of yellow teeth on metal spoon and words Green Giant. Ivor open them for Tall Nole and Droo.

'And me,' say Arron.

Ivor go back to fridge and see it have no more Green Giant. He shake hims head. Arron tcha. Droo have already eat some yellow teeth but offer tin to Arron. Arron tcha again. Tall Nole have not eat yet but do not offer.

'Yum yum,' he say as he dip fingers in tin.

'You have long journey back to Kimry?' say Jims.

'Far enough,' say Effan.

Arron watch as Tall Nole and Droo eat. Tall Nole do not eat quiet. As he finish, he use hims fingers to get out all that is left.

'Yum yum yum,' he say.

Ivor bring three more tinfoods. All is also different from before. All have yellow paper with pictures of white lumps in glop. He put them on the table between brothers and Tall Nole and Droo.

Of a sudden, all reach for them. Tall Nole and Arron is first, then Effan. Nino and Droo is without. Jims smile at Tall Nole.

'We is all friends. Give,' he say.

Tall Nole do as is ask and hand tin to Nino. Brothers drink beer, finish tinfoods, belch.

'Time to go now. I wish you safe journey,' say Jims.

He stand. Brothers stand.

'Safe journey,' say Droo.

Arron hand beer bottle to Tall Nole.

'For you,' he say.

Tall Nole drink from bottle and find it is empty.

'Yum yum,' say Arron.

And now it all go pigsarse. Tall Nole headbutt Arron so hard he fall to floor. Other brothers rush him. Kicks, punches, elbows, heads, spits, hair grabs, bites. Arron get up and join in also.

'Stop,' say Jims.

'Stop,' say Droo.

All the brothers have guns but keep them over thems backs. Howul look for chance to grab one but it do not hap. Only one time in hims life can he take on three Padded Men and win.

For now he watch as blood spray and teeth fly. At last three is too much for one. Effan sit on Tall Noles chest, Nino sit on hims legs and Arron spit in hims face. Then all stand up.

'We must go now,' say Effan.

'Wait,' say Jims as they walk to door.

Arron tcha. Effan shush him.

'You need them with you,' say Jims.

He nod at Droo and Tall Nole.

'We know way,' say Effan.

'They have Big Keys,' say Jims. 'They go with you, isnit?'

Now all is smiles and forgive. Except for Tall Nole who poison Arron with hims eyes.

'All is good now, yes?' say Jims.

'Yes,' say Droo.

'Yes,' say Effan.

'Yes,' say Nino.

'Yes,' say Arron.

Tall Nole say nothing.

'Nole?' say Jims.

'Yes,' say Tall Nole.

They leave but Ivor do not go with them. Perhaps they

forget him. Scanks is easy to forget. One more nor less do not matter. Or perhap they just prefer to be on thems own.

Now it is just Howul, Ivor, Jims.

'Sit,' Jims say.

Like others before, he offer Howul a way out.

'Help me and I promise you is safe,' he say.

Howul know what this mean. Such a good, kind man. Different. Someone I must help. Like fuckery.

He know it is more of the same. Mister Jims will talk to him, try to get from him all he know, hurt him or give him more tinfoods then, if he do not scape first, kill him.

Mister Jims throw questions –

'How many people in Kimry?'

'How many guns?'

'Is Brenin well like?'

'Do everyone in Kimry have plenty food?'

Blanow and Kimry is more connect than Howul ever dream. But still plenty is Do they and Is he and How many. Jims want answers. Brenins alway want answers. Howul do not give them.

'I mean it,' say Jim. 'Tell me what you know and you is safe.'

'Safe as Yorath. Safe as my daughter.'

Mister Jims tcha.

'Say what you do after you leave here.'

'I kill seven sea monisters, dob thirteen women then become Brenin in a village where tinfoods grow on trees.'

'Still you is most big arsepain in Blanow. I give you chance. Why you not take it?'

'You kill my daughter.'

'No I do not. We can be good for each other. You can have all you need. Tell me.'

Howul tell nothing. He and Jims sit in silence. Ivor, as per the usual, stand in silence. Then something most strange hap.

'I can help you,' say a soft, weak, quiet, high voice.

Ivors voice. He throw Mister Jims hims own best creep smile. My son learn quick, think Howul.

'I is in Kimry far more long than Howul,' say Ivor. 'I can tell you all. How many guns, how many people, how much food.'

'I do not ask you,' say Jims.

'Also, I have this,' say Ivor.

He loose a rag round hims arm and free from it four small brown medicine bottles, like those Loyd use.

'These is special medicines I bring for you. They is from Kimry. They is best.'

My boy, think Howul.

After Howul leave, main go-tos for sick people in Blanow is Timmo and Pat. Both kill more than they heal. Jims pick up a bottle.

'What is?' he say.

'It heal blight. And bad heart. And bad nerves.'

Jims pick up another.

'This?'

'Typho. Thick throat. Body stones.'

'And this?'

'Blood clots. Corruptions. Cramps. Ulcers. Swell up stomach.'

Dont overdo, think Howul. Hims boy is smart but still have much to learn. Make it matter even more to Jims. Offer him what he need himself.

Howul remember Jims stiff fingers and bad knees. He pick up Ivors last bottle.

'This heal stiff fingers and bad knees,' he say.

'For sure?'

'For sure.'

Howul give him bottle. He is about to drink some then stop. He give it to Ivor to taste first. Ivor taste, smile and hand back. Jims drink. It taste bad so it must be good.

Howul now realise what he should have realise before. Droo and Tall Nole will return soon but right now it is just him, Ivor, Jims.

As Jims put the bottle down he sense something have change.

'Others is back soon,' he say. 'If you want tinfoods, you can take. We have our differences, Howul. But now as Brenin what I say matter. What I have decide is this. You can both stay here and be safe. I give you full pardon.'

Honey words to keep him quiet till Tall Nole and Droo return. Then safe as Yorath. Safe as Erin. Drown. Throw from High Rock. Both of them.

He believe I is same as before, think Howul. Do nothing.

Say nothing. Accept. Suffer. Be stupid. Not no more. Time to give back.

Jims give creep smile and reach for something in hims People Before black coat. Quick as blink, Howul push over the table between them. Tinfoods and bottles fall onto Jims lap. As he try to clear them, Howul pick up wood chair and smash it over hims head.

'Do not watch this,' Howul say to Ivor.

He do as hims father say. He leave the room.

Jims groan and sit up. What he have get from hims coat is on floor beside him with tinfoods and bottles. Small. Make of metal. Less big, less long but still a gun.

Howul kick all away and smash him over head again. Then he go to the gun, pick it up and point it. Jims watch, wait, say nothing. No honey words now. And from Howul, no forgive.

'You know Erin is too young for Challenge. Why you let it hap?'

'Yorath is Brenin. I cannot stop Brenin.'

'You have not want to stop him.'

'Of course I have. I get rid of him. I make bad things good.'

'The two babys you just send to Kimry. This is good?'

'It is what must be, isnit? But with you I will change it.'

Blood boil in Howuls brain. All that have hap to him. All the bad things he do and have do to him. And now this. Shitebag tell him it is right that hims daughter is kill, hims brothers take from him, hims son take from him.

He push gun against Jims head.

Stones and pebbles have shout at him. Screams and blood have fill hims sleep. Sweat and shakes wake him still. Kill do not mend, Featherwoman say. Kill alway make more bad.

With the others, he kill them to scape. This is different. If he kill Jims, he do it for anger and hate.

He call for hims son. Ivor return.

'I cannot do it,' he say.

'Good,' say Ivor.

'Find rope or wire to tie him.'

Ivor leave again and return soon with both and knife to cut with. Together they tie Jims firm to chair with rope and turn table back over. Then wait for Tall Nole and Droo to return.

Howul know he still have to kill them. No choice. What

must be. But he do not want to kill them in front of Ivor.

'I must go find them,' he say.

'I go with,' say Ivor.

'It is not safe.'

'No mind.'

'I need you here. To watch him. You have knife. Use it if you must.'

He say this more for Jims than Ivor but still worry how it sound. He do not want hims son to kill people.

'Try not to use it,' he say.

Before he leave, he go over to fridge and get some tinfoods for Ivor. Inside he see Green Giant tins with yellow teeth, yellow tins with white lumps in glop on them. Ivor have pretend there is none to set brothers and Tall Nole against each other.

Howul go over to him, hug him.

'You is good son,' he say. 'You save us.'

Ivor do not push him away. He hug him back. Tears pinch Howuls eyes. To rid them, he get bizzy. He cross the room so huge you can throw clodge and not reach far wall with it. He go out of front door and head for Field of Black. As he do this, he see someone come toward him from there. This person walk slow and stumble like he is sick. Droo. Howul call hims name. Droo stop and do not answer.

Howul hurry over to him but still with gun in hand. Droos chest have blood over it. Howul take hims arm, help him back to Big House and lay him on floor. Droo is cold with shock. Howul ask Ivor to bring blankets. Then he use knife to cut piece from Jims black coat and push this down hard on chest to stop bleed.

'What hap?' say Jims.

'In tunnel Tall Nole say they only win because they is three against one.'

'Dont talk, Droo,' say Howul.

Ivor return with blankets and put them over Droo. Still Droo want to talk.

'Tall Nole say he fight them one by one. One of them want this but others tell him No. Tall Nole call them yelly bellys, go over to first and throw punch. Others take guns off thems backs and shoot him. Something hit me also.'

'Stop, Droo. Tell us when you is well.'

'We is not at first door yet so they take Big Keys from us and move on. They have Big Keys.'

Howul press more. The blood slow but do not stop. He know he cannot save Droo but say soft words, encourage, hold hims hand. When hims eyes close, they do not open again.

Tall Nole dead, Droo dead, brothers away. Jims cannot hurt them now.

'Stay here and wait,' say Howul to him. 'If you try to leave, I make sure there is trial. You do not want trial, isnit?'

'No,' say Jims.

Howul now take Ivor from room to room in Big House. He say it is to make sure no one else is there but, for true, he want to keep bizzy because he is so freak by all that have hap. Also, he want to see what Brenin Blanow have.

Everything in the rooms is clean and neat, like Jack and Julie live here. And most things is of People Before.

In one room there is just books. Some is big with long names like Newnes Pictorial Knowledge An Educational Treasury And Children's Dictionary, Cassells Natural History and the Oxford Illustrated Dictionary. Some is all just words, some also have pictures of flutterbys and birds and ants and fish and People Before in strange clothes and with strange items make by them.

A few is books like Howul have find in Rids house. Pictures of People Before women with fall off clothes. Howul put them under other books so Ivor will not see them.

He find also the red box Gommel have give him. Inside still is the CURE OF EVERY FORM OF DISEASE book.

Next to the box is teeny books Gommel have give others to write in. A big pile of them with many teeny words in them. What hap in Blanow. What people say and do. For instance Today Kaydor tell Bonny she is greedygus and take pattycake from her but Gerrun tell Kaydor he will tell Rona so Kaydor give pattycake back to Bonny who say Kaydor have mess it with dirt and she is not greedygus. Pages and pages and pages fill with other peoples dribble. Then, every so oft, a few words about him. How grumpscrut he is, how he make snotnose Lorunse cry, how he annoy Milani, how he say Reeta is sick after she give him pattycake. He do not know who write them but Gommel must have learn some others also. So Brenin can know what hap. Reeta and Si, most like.

One room have only food in it. Tinfoods of course but also meat of chicken and pigeon and rat and ripe fruit and vegetables of all kinds and pattycakes and eggs and dry fish.

Five rooms have only People Before clothes and shoes and hats. So many that, even if you wear same thing only for two year, still you die many time before you have wear them all.

All through the house is things Howul do not know what is for. A bottle of black liquid that stain teeth and taste so bad he spit it out. A small piece of clear plasty with numbers on. A big piece of white plasty shape like a bird. A big round piece of wood same shape as a thumb with picture of old woman on it. It open and inside is a more small piece of wood with picture of less old woman on it then inside more small, less old, more small, less old till there is baby. Point of picture is that you see it. Why have one picture that hide nineteen other?

No matter. For the moment, all is good again. He will be Blanow Brenin after all. He will make changes. Special. Except now he also remember what Droo have say. The brothers take with them the Big Keys. Keys that keep lock the two metal doors that connect Blanow with Tangrish and make everyone safe from People Outside. People Outside is no more lock out. Blanow is lock in.

#

This is all else I have of Forse that Howul write. He tell me that, when others tell it, some time Sky beat Deep and save Prinsess. Some time Deep regret bad things he have do and change or kill himself. Some time Sky go bad and join Deep. This is how Howul end it.

FORSE

Liteblade is strong in Skys hand. All he wish of it hap. Spin left. Push forwid. Throw fire at Deeps hart. But every where he strike, air is all he wound. Deep know all he do before he do it. Like gulls that fly neer, round, under, over and never tutch wings, every time Sky wish hurt, Deep step away, stay safe.

Most time Deep distroy like all is mud he wipe from hand. But he throw no fire at Sky.

Platform they stand on shake, creek. Black mettul over Deeps face stop Sky from see into eyes, reed mind.

Skys legs, arms is now water. Bad thinkings take over. Of blood Deep have spill. Terror he have make. Of what Prinsess suffer now, what more she must suffer. He can not help nor save her. Liteblade fall from hand.

Now at last Deeps liteblade throw fire at Sky, hit ground in frunt of him. He step back. More fire, more step back, more fire, more step back till Sky is neer edje of platform. Beyond is dark air, space.

'Yoo is brave. Strong. Join me,' say Deep.

He reach black glove forwid to pull Sky to him, make him safe.

Sky pick up liteblade insted.

Deep do not stop him.

Skys liteblade move, twist, spin, throw fire. Deep push out chest, stand tall, let fire hit him. Feerce heet, wite hot flames. On Deep, soft as womans kiss.

Liteblade grow hevvy, fall from Skys hand again.

'No choice,' say Deep. 'Join me.'

'Never,' say Sky. 'All I want or love yoo have kill.'

'I spare yoo.'

'To hurt me more. To show me what else yoo distroy.'

'No. Yoo do not know it but I is same as yoo.'

'As same as rock and water.'

'Kind is not brave, Sky. Good is not strong. Forse is best. Join me. Then there is forse none can stop. Yoo know where yor father is?

'Kill by yoo. Safe in jentle erth.'

Deep lift up black mettul. Eyes behind is as black, as dark.

'Yor father stand before yoo now.'

More pain than of thousand liteblades tare at Sky.

'Never true,' he say.

'Admit. Accept. Join me.'

Deep offer hand again for Sky to take. Sky do not. He step back insted. Turn. And jump.

#

All in Blanow have now see Big House, Field of Black and the tunnel that lead to Tangrish. Many have lose thems own babys this way. They cry for them.

Any day more Padded Men will return and do to them what brothers do to Tall Nole and Droo. Only way to be safe is to collapse tunnel or fill it with rocks. They begin to fill with rocks but it is slow.

They blame Jims for babys, Field of Black and tunnel. Anything else they blame on Howul. So when he tell them he is now Brenin and will make bad things good, they tcha and say they prefer to be eat by sea monisters than this. Some want trial for Jims. Some want trial for Jims and Howul. Some want trial for those who put less rocks in tunnel than they do. With no Brenin, everything fall apart. The Green become place with no fire where everyone argue and fight.

Treva say he will not go to Place for Lookout no more and will instead look after chickens. Gale say she is fed up with pull out weeds and will also look after chickens. Kim and Crayg who look after chickens tell them both to gofuck. Reeta say she have pains that mean she cannot work no more. Big Tris say she will now only make pattycakes for herself.

Glend bring back bones from Field of Black she say is her man Jerrys. Si tell her they is bones of hims woman Dee. Glend scream so long at him he no more care if they is

Jerrys, Dees nor old tree branches.

Then Eddy think of something to stop Padded Men from return. He say he can heat up metal and fill lock with it. This will keep the first door in tunnel from open and make them safe. Ken say if the Padded Men cannot open the door they will be even more angry. When they find other way in, they will come back and kill everyone for sure. Treva say Ken is stupid and have not listen. Padded Men cannot kill anyone if they is lock out. Glend tcha every time anyone speak.

All talk at same time till Andi tell everyone to shut up and Si and Gale and Kim tell Andi to shut up for tell them to shut up. While all this hap, Eddy go off and fill lock with hot metal.

When he return, he say no one can ever open door again. No more fret nor fright. Everyone thank him. Glend hug him, cry on hims shoulder and say she have alway think he should be Brenin. Eddy say he do not want to be Brenin and say Si should be Brenin. Si say he will be Brenin but then Gale and Kim say they dont want him. Everyone say who they think will make good Brenin. Andi is upset because no one say him, Ken because some say him and others dont, Crayg because Glend will not shut up when he want to say something and Glend because, no matter how many time she say Eddy is best Brenin, Si, Ken and Andi do not agree. Howul say nothing because he know no one will listen.

Eddy become new Brenin.

#

The most old man in Blanow sit in bed with cushion for hims back and cloth under hims chin to catch spit and dribble. Like for Loyd, one side of hims face now do not move when rest of it do. Back of hims head have bad shape where Howul have crush it with stick.

He cannot walk nor lift hims arms. Hims teeth is fall out. Hims eyes is weak. No smell nor feel nor taste. But he still live.

'Why. You. Here?' he say.

He push each word out slow and fight for more breath between. The words shake and slide as he speak them. Every time he make one, it is like he make it for first time.

'There is something you must tell me,' say Howul. 'Who kill my daughter?'

Nothing.

'Who kill Erin?'

Nothing.

'You kill her?'

Nothing.

'Who?'

Nothing.

'Tall Nole?'

Nothing.

'Who?'

Nothing.

'You feel bad for what you do?'

Nothing.

So much of him is brack already. What else can Howul still do to make him speak? He stand up and go to the big chair Gommel sit in before. He use hims shoulder to barge it away so the black + mark show. He press with hims foot. The plank lift up. He reach inside.

In there is the two books. Jack and Julie Learn To Read and The A B C Book. He take them out. He read to Gommel of Neville and hims anorak, Mary and Uncle Jims stamps, Dulcie and her jolly sailor. Then he get a light candle from its stand and hold it close to the shiny snotnoses on the cover.

'Books is dangerous,' say Howul.

'No,' say Gommel.

Howul move the flame more close. Some glop catch fire.

'Stop,' say Gommel.

Howul rub the fire out with hims thumb.

'Who kill her?' he say.

Gommel shake hims head.

'Tell me who.'

Howul move candle toward book again. Gommel try to speak and start to cough. More glop catch fire.

'Stop,' say Gommel.

Howul spit on Jack and Julie Learn To Read and put out fire.

'Tell me,' say Howul.

'Daughter.'

'Yes.'

He sit there old and weak, eyes wet from book smoke. Hims chest jump with every try for breath. Each word is heavy rock to push.

'She. Kill. Self.'

He say this to hurt me back, think Howul. Of course Erin do not kill herself. Tall Nole kill her. Or Jims. Or Droo. Or Gommel.

'Tell me true,' he say and hold flame to book again.

'True,' say Gommel.

Howul move Jack and Julie Learn To Read round in hims hands so each part catch. Gommel watch and say nothing. There is much smoke. Oft time fire go out. Howul put flame to it again and again. Gommel cough many time but still do not speak.

Evil old slimefuck lie to me, think Howul. Then he remember what he keep bury so long. What Milani say of Erin when he describe her grief since Jen die.

'Perhaps she want to die also,' she say.

After Jen is kill in cyclone, alway Erin have hungry and cold. Do not eat, no friends. Crap father. Age fourteen, she is White Dress Woman. They give her to Tall Nole. Her life is make so bad she no more want it.

He have promise Jen he will take care of her. He have fail.

Glend say same as Gommel.

'I find her in The Senter,' she say. 'She hang herself with ribbon. I free her, lay her on the ground. Then Jims and Droo take her away. Most sad. But life is sad, isnit?'

When first he write in the books Gommel give him, he think this help him. Make hims mind clear. Understand what he mean and think. Understand what others mean and think. But now he know different. When he burn Jack and Julie Learn To Read, this help him more. It make him feel even more good. To write is complicate. To burn is simple. Complicate just bring pain.

Why it take him so long to see this? Of course, isnit. What people say is true. Books fill your head with dribble. Instead of help Erin, he read Jack and Julie and think about anoraks and jelly. Too bizzy with books, he have let her die. Without them, he will have save her.

To hims crap house with concrete floor, fall down walls and no roof, he have bring Newnes Pictorial Knowledge An

Educational Treasury And Children's Dictionary, Cassells Natural History and the Oxford Illustrated Dictionary, hims own teeny books, the teeny books in Big House fill with what hap in Blanow, the CURE OF EVERY FORM OF DISEASE book hims father give him, the books scanks in Kimry get him, the women with fall off clothes books. They do not put roof on hims house nor stop cyclone from blow down walls. They do not keep Erin from die.

He push bricks together and light a fire inside them. As alway for him, the wood spit and bubble and do not want to stay light.

He tear pages out of CURE OF EVERY FORM OF DISEASE and throw them in.

They have damp, burn slow and do not give good heat.

Burn all of them. If he is Brenin, if he do great things, if he have great story, hims words count. But he have no story. He do nothing. He know shite about shite.

This is why he is save and what hims life is for. To burn every write down word he find.

There is many pages and he have to rip each out to get it to light. Some time he stop and read again before he throw them in. Adipose tissue. Bile. Coma. Dysentery. Excrescences. Fracture. Gofuck.

When I find him, plenty have burn and other books is pile up, ready to go next.

'Can I have them?' I say.

He do not want to give them to me.

'You can read?' he say.

'Not yet. You will learn me?'

He do not want to. But what else can he do? He is my father. This is first thing I ask him for. I keep the books. He learn me to read and write.

#

AFTER

If Howuls story is like those he tell, you find out now all else that is for true. Have Tegwin know that Griff send him to Blanow only to be punish? Howul alway think so. I do not. It is difference we have.

Shut in Blanow, Howul cannot learn what hap to her nor Catrin, Beth, Loyd, Featherwoman, Rid, Griff etcetera etcetera. He is not Sky nor Gladilator nor even Sissypuss. He is, he say, man who go where others have not go, see what others have not see, do what others have not do and make a right pigsarse of all of it.

I tell hims story different. He is man who lose those he love most and still hate himself every day for not do more to save them. I see the good things he have do, the bad things he have stop. He do not.

Now the most old man in Blanow, he never have woman nor man again and never try Challenge again. Hims legs is become less good, hims eyes more weak. Others watch from Place for Lookout, make potch and is go-to for heal. He complain about them and all else. How thiefy and greedy and stupid all is. He is become so craxy everyone avoid him. Except me. Every day I give him time for at least one complain before urgent bizzy take me away.

No Padded Men have ever return here. Yet.

In Blanow, there is no Ulderun, Prinsess nor lightblades. No defiance nor brave soldiers nor glory deaths. No trees that talk nor birds that die for love. Here is mess, greed, fear, struggle, worry, spite, hate, say one thing and do another, say too little, say too much, steal, argue, lie, hurt. This is what Howul see. There is also love, share, help, kind, accept, enjoy. What I see.

Because of Howul I is no more red rags skinbone in Kimry. For me, scratchy, messy life in Blanow is still sweet. Because of him.

When fever remove Mister Eddy and hims woman Milani, new Brenin try to give everyone more and share more. If people die, oft time there is no Challenge and no new life. If baby arrive that should not, it live but Challenge is delay even more. Even high ups now have same food as others. It is enough but still people complain. Maddy have more big pattycake or potato, Brin find scrag and do not share, Rishart have take Erryanwens apple while she sleep. They forget how hungry they is before.

New Brenin have new thing he do. Big thing no Brenin ever do before. Words is precious to him. Without them, life is fog and fuddle. So he make sure everyone is learn how to read and write. He believe it fill thems minds more and mean they complain less. Howul tell him they complain same. They just have more words to complain with.

There is still one secret new Blanow Brenin keep to himself.

As a scank snotnose who is small for hims age, he have know only one thing of hims time before he reach Kimry. How old he is when he leave Blanow. If Erin still live, she is same age as him. She is no twin.

He know for sure Howul is not hims father. So who is? Most like another craxy arsepain grumpscrut with nose big enough for snotnoses to hide under. Most like Rid.

Howul like to think that he is good father to me and I is good son. So much else is take from him. I do not take that.

My name is change now.

Idris, not Ivor.

Mister Idris.

THE END

ACKNOWLEDGEMENTS

As I am now incredibly old – even older than Howul – the number of people who in my time have helped me with my writing is huge. Without them, no Howul. Rather than list them all individually, I'm just providing first names. If you think I mean you, I do. (Thank you, Martin South). If you aren't sure I mean you, I probably still do (thank you Adrian Poole, Andrew Martin, Anne Boston, Pat Garratt). Some go back a very long way (thank you Brian Worthington, thank you Douglas Henderson). Some apply to several different people. Some are people who aren't with us anymore. And some I've omitted. Forgetful, not ungrateful.

Adam, Adrian, Aki, Al, Allan, All those Shannons again, Andrew, Angus, Anna, Anne, Benji, Bernardine the Mighty and Magnificent, Bob, Brenda, Brian, Carol, Cassandra, Dixon, Douglas, Ed *and* Michael, Emma Jay, Florence, Graham, Harry, Hilary, James, Jane, Janet, Joe, Jonny, Julia, Larry, Lawrence, Lindsay, Maggie, Marc, Marcelle, Martin, Miles, Nic, Noelle, Oli, Onuora, Pat, Paul, Penny, Peta, Pete, Peter, Sam, Sarah, Sofia, Steve, Sue.

Special thanks to all at the Literary Consultancy for your help, encouragement and invaluable practical advice; to Peter and Alison at Elsewhen for saying Yes when others said No and for all your wisdom, good humour, patience and support; to Oli and Florence at A M Heath for also taking a chance on me; to all the amazing LARPers and Freeformers who have not just put up with but even encouraged my strange antics over the years; to previous storytellers whose reflected glory I'm shamelessly basking in (Homer, Catullus, Oscar Wilde); and to the creators of Star Wars for providing a fable as stirring as any that generations before it could muster.

David Shannon
November 2020

HOWLISH – ENGLISH

Some parts of this book are written in an older version of Howlish. Its idiosyncracies aren't listed here. There are plenty of them but they won't (I hope) be too hard to work out. Some also occur in the newer version of Howlish which the rest of the book uses. These include:

- Third person singulars are always third person plurals. Has is always Have, Wants is always Want, etc. The one exception is the word to be. Is always replaces Are and Am.

- Present, future and past tenses are often the same. For instance, "allow" can mean "allow", "will allow" or "allowed", "satisfy" can mean "satisfy", "will satisfy" or "satisfied".

- The context should make clear which tense a verb is. To avoid confusion, "will" and "have" can also be used as in "have allow," "will allow", etc..

- Some verbs are used as nouns, too, so "amaze" is also "amazement", "punish" is also "punishment".

- With some words, the plural and singular are the same. Season means "a single season" or "seasons", Year means "a single year" or "years".

- Adjectives and adverbs are often the same. "Usual" is "usual" and "usually", "quick" is "quick" and "quickly".

- "The" and "a" are often used with nouns but are sometimes dropped. There is no "an".

- "Hims" replaces "his" but can sometimes replace "its", too.

- Some words are changed but close enough to what they were before for you to understand (I hope). A "hallooshanin" is a hallucination, a "flutterby" is a butterfly, etc.

- A few words are completely new. They are listed and defined below.

  brenin = chief

  chuffy = annoyingly cheerful

  craxy = tetchy

  daggy = messed up

  dob = have sex with

  grooly = ugly

  keriss = beautiful

  Madbad = a person from Blanow

  potch = mixture

  scrunty = ugly

  shonked = ruined

  shooky = worst of the worst

  stiffneck disease = tetanus

  thick throat = diptheria

Elsewhen Press

delivering outstanding new talents in speculative fiction

Visit the Elsewhen Press website at elsewhen.press for the latest information on all of our titles, authors and events; to read our blog; find out where to buy our books and ebooks; or to place an order.

Sign up for the Elsewhen Press InFlight Newsletter at elsewhen.press/newsletter

THE EYE COLLECTORS

A STORY OF
HER MAJESTY'S OFFICE OF THE WITCHFINDER GENERAL
PROTECTING THE PUBLIC FROM THE UNNATURAL SINCE 1645

SIMON KEWIN

When Danesh Shahzan gets called to a crime scene, it's usually because the police suspect not just foul play but unnatural forces at play.

Danesh is an Acolyte in Her Majesty's Office of the Witchfinder General, a shadowy arm of the British government fighting supernatural threats to the realm. This time, he's been called in by Detective Inspector Nikola Zubrasky to investigate a murder in Cardiff. The victim had been placed inside a runic circle and their eyes carefully removed from their head. Danesh soon confirms that magical forces are at work. Concerned that there may be more victims to come, he and DI Zubrasky establish a wary collaboration as they each pursue the investigation within the constraints of their respective organisations. Soon Danesh learns that there may be much wider implications to what is taking place and that somehow he has an unexpected connection. He also realises something about himself that he can never admit to the people with whom he works…

"Think *Dirk Gently* meets *Good Omens!*"

ISBN: 9781911409748 (epub, kindle) / ISBN: 9781911409649 (288pp paperback)

Visit bit.ly/TheEyeCollectors

Bloodsworn

Book 1 of the Avatars of Ruin

Tej Turner

"Classic epic fantasy. I enjoyed it enormously"
– Anna Smith Spark

Everyone from Jalard knew what a bloodoath was. Legendary characters in tales they were told as children made such pacts with the gods. By drawing one's own blood whilst making a vow, such people became 'Bloodsworn'. And in every tale where the oath was broken, the ending was always the same. The Bloodsworn died.

It has been twelve years since The War of Ashes, but animosity still lingers between the nations of Sharma and Gavendara, and only a few souls have dared to cross the border between them.

The villagers of Jalard live a simplistic life, tucked away in the hills of western Sharma and far away from the boundary which was once a warzone. To them tales of bloodshed seem no more than distant fables. They have little contact with the outside world, apart from once a year when they are visited by representatives from the Academy who choose two of them to be taken away to their institute in the capital. To be Chosen is considered a great honour… of which most of Jalard's children dream.

But this year the Academy representatives make an announcement which is so shocking it causes friction between the villagers and some of them begin to suspect that all is not what it seems. Just where are they taking the Chosen, and why? Some of them seek to find out, but what they find will change their lives forever and set them on a path seeking vengeance…

ISBN: 9781911409779 (epub, kindle) / ISBN: 9781911409670 (432pp paperback)

Visit bit.ly/Bloodsworn

THE RHYMER

an Heredyssey

DOUGLAS THOMPSON

The Rhymer, an Heredyssey defies classification in any one literary genre. A satire on contemporary society, particularly the art world, it is also a comic-poetic meditation on the nature of life, death and morality.

A mysterious tramp wanders from town to town, taking a new name and identity from whoever he encounters first. Apparently amnesiac or even brain-damaged, Nadith Learmot nonetheless has other means to access the past and perhaps even the future: upon his chest a dial, down his sleeves wires that he can connect to the walls of old buildings from which he believes he can read their ghosts like imprints on tape. Haunting him constantly is the resemblance he apparently bears to his supposed brother, a successful artist called Zenir. Setting out to pursue Zenir and denounce or blackmail him out of spite, in his travels around the satellite towns and suburbs surrounding a city called Urbis, Nadith finds he is always two steps behind a figure as enigmatic and polyfaceted as himself. But through second hand snippets of news he increasingly learns of how his brother's fortunes are waning, while his own, to his surprise, are on the rise. Along the way, he encounters unexpected clues to his own true identity, how he came to lose his memory and acquire his strange 'contraption'. When Nadith finally catches up with Zenir, what will they make of each other?

Told entirely in the first person in a rhythmic stream of lyricism, Nadith's story reads like Shakespeare on acid, leaving the reader to guess at the truth that lies behind his madness. Is Nadith a mental health patient or a conman? ... Or as he himself comes to believe, the reincarnation of the thirteenth century Scottish seer True Thomas The Rhymer, a man who never lied nor died but disappeared one day to return to the realm of the faeries who had first given him his clairvoyant gifts?

ISBN: 9781908168511 (epub, kindle) / ISBN: 9781908168412 (192pp paperback)
Visit bit.ly/TheRhymer-Heredyssey

THE MAREK SERIES BY JULIET KEMP
BOOK 1:
THE DEEP AND SHINING DARK
A Locus Recommended Read in 2018

"A rich and memorable tale of political ambition, family and magic, set in an imagined city that feels as vibrant as the characters inhabiting it."
Aliette de Bodard
Nebula-award winning author of *The Tea Master and the Detective*

You know something's wrong when the cityangel turns up at your door

Magic within the city-state of Marek works without the need for bloodletting, unlike elsewhere in Teren, thanks to an agreement three hundred years ago between an angel and the founding fathers. It also ensures that political stability is protected from magical influence. Now, though, most sophisticates no longer even believe in magic *or* the cityangel.

But magic has suddenly stopped working, discovers Reb, one of the two sorcerers who survived a plague that wiped out virtually all of the rest. Soon she is forced to acknowledge that someone has deposed the cityangel without being able to replace it. Marcia, Heir to House Fereno, and one of the few in high society who is well-aware that magic still exists, stumbles across that same truth. But it is just one part of a much more ambitious plan to seize control of Marek.

Meanwhile, city Council members connive and conspire, unaware that they are being manipulated in a dangerous political game. A game that threatens the peace and security not just of the city, but all the states around the Oval Sea, including the shipboard traders of Salina upon whom Marek relies.

To stop the impending disaster, Reb and Marcia, despite their difference in status, must work together alongside the deposed cityangel and Jonas, a messenger from Salina. But first they must discover who is behind the plot, and each of them must try to decide who they can really trust.

ISBN: 9781911409342 (epub, kindle) / ISBN: 9781911409243 (272pp paperback)
Visit bit.ly/DeepShiningDark

BOOK 2:
SHADOW AND STORM

"never short on adventure and intrigue... the characters are real, full of depth, and richly drawn, and you'll wish you had even more time with them by book's end. A fantastic read."
Rivers Solomon
Author of *An Unkindness of Ghosts*, Lambda, Tiptree and Locus finalist

Never trust a demon... or a Teren politician

The annual visit by the Teren Throne's representative, the Lord Lieutenant, is merely a symbolic gesture. But this year the Lieutenant has been unexpectedly replaced and Marcia, Heir to House Fereno, suspects a new agenda.

Teren magic is enabled by bloodletting. A Teren magician will invoke a demon and bind them with blood. But demons are devious and if unleashed are sure to create havoc. The Teren way to stop them involves the letting of more of the magician's blood – often terminally. But if a young magician is being sought by an unleashed demon, their only hope may be to escape to Marek where the cityangel can keep the demon at bay. Probably.

Once again Reb, Cato, Jonas and Beckett must deal with a magical problem, while Marcia must tackle a serious political challenge to Marek's future.

ISBN: 9781911409595 (epub, kindle) / ISBN: 9781911409496 (336pp paperback)
Visit bit.ly/ShadowAndStorm

ABOUT DAVID SHANNON

David Shannon grew up in Bristol, the youngest of 3 children. Yes, he was the spoilt one. After stints as a TEFL teacher in Italy and croupier in London, he had a first writing career as a journalist working for (among others) *Cosmopolitan*, the *Sunday Times*, the *Radio Times*, *Good Housekeeping*, *Country Living* and *Best*. He wrote a lot about showbiz, interviewing and profiling many celebrities.

Even though any actors he met kept telling him what a difficult career theirs is, he then abandoned journalism for acting. Many years later he's still doing it, using the name David France. How successful has he been at this? Judge for yourself. Have you ever heard of him? He's done plenty of low-budget feature films (including *Werewolves of the Third Reich*) but makes most of his living by writing, running and acting in murder mystery events.

Chronic shyness afflicted him for many years but he is now painfully opinionated about almost everything. And he loves pigs. Despite this, he remains happily married to a writer slightly more famous than him – the 2019 Booker Prize winner, Bernardine Evaristo. They live in London.